AF572382

The Tarnished Halo

Padre Francisco Hidalgo

Robert F. Carter

The Tarnished Halo

The Story of Padre Francisco Hidalgo

FRANCISCAN HERALD PRESS
Chicago, Illinois 60609

Library of Congress Cataloging in Publication Data:

Carter, Robert F.
The Tarnished Halo

Bibliography: 170 pages
1. Hidalgo, Francisco, 1659? - 1726. 2. Indians of North America — Texas — Missions. 3. Indians of Mexico — Missions. I. Title.
E78.T4C37 266'.2'0924 [B] 73-8669
ISBN 0-8199-0457-0

Chicago, Illinois 60609.
Printed in the United States of America
First Edition

Dedicated to the memory
of
Friar Francisco Hidalgo and his colleagues,
who did so much to shape the destiny
of
Texas, the United States, and Mexico.

Author's Foreword

As a native Texan and descendant of a pioneer family, I have been fascinated for many years by the brief glimpses in conventional histories of Friar Francisco Hidalgo and his part in the founding of the first missions in Texas and several in northern Mexico. When I was finally able to devote some time to a study of the source material, my interest grew, but even more so did my amazement that such a character and such a story had received such casual treatment by historians.

Even in histories printed for use in Texas, the story is alloted only three or four paragraphs. Yet Francisco Hidalgo not only preceded the highly publicized Junípero Serra of California fame, and Eusebio Kino who worked in Arizona, but his story is even more dramatic and the impact of his work even more important.

These facts and the realization of the great influence of his efforts on the development of Texas, the United States, and Mexico, to say nothing of Spain and France, persuaded me to try, as best I could, to bring him more into the public notice.

Included in an appendix are translations of eight previously unpublished letters of Friar Francisco Hidalgo dated May 17, 1704; September 8, 1706; October 9, 1706; July 22, 1716; October 6, 1716; April 18, 1718; November 3, 1723; May 29, 1724.

These letters are included through the courtesy of Fr. Marion A. Habig O.F.M., of the Franciscan Herald Press, and Fr. Benedict Leutenegger O.F.M., of the Research Library at Mission San José in San Antonio, Texas. The translation is also by Fr. Leutenegger.

I am most grateful for the privilege of including these letters.

CONTENTS

Author's Foreword vii
Publisher's Note xiii
1. Hidalgo's Dream 3
2. A First Step 11
3. A Fateful Shipwreck 17
4. A Dream Comes True 23
5. Hidalgo's Vow 33
6. The Road Back 41
7. A Sly Trick 49
8. At San Juan Bautista 57
9. Life in a Frontier Mission 63
10. The Guardian 73
11. Treason! 83
12. The French React 93
13. Hidalgo and St. Denis 101
14. The Return 107
15. History Repeats 113
16. War! 123
17. Ebb Tide 129
Bibliography 135
Appendix: Letters of Fr. Hidalgo 137
1. Letter of May 17, 1704 137
2. Letter of September 8, 1706 139
3. Letter of October 9, 1706 141
4. Letter of July 22, 1716 143
5. Letter of October 6, 1716 147
6. Letter of April 18, 1718 150
7. Letter of November 3, 1723 152
8. Letter of May 29, 1724 158

List of Illustrations and Maps

San Francisco Mission — 26
First Mission East Texas — 27
San Bernardo Mission — 55
Doorway to the Courtyard — 59
Early Missionary Work — 66
San Juan Bautista Missions — 67
Interior of the Church — 72
Querétaro College — 76
French Louisiana — 116
East Texas Missions 1716 — 117
The Alamo — 121
Typical Mission — 131

Publisher's Note

Robert F. Carter is a retired lawyer and Naval officer (captain). He has been awarded the Legion of Merit, with two citations, the Reserve Medal, with star, and numerous campaign medals. As a lawyer he served on the staff of the General Attorney of a major oil company in various posts in the United States and Latin America.

Captain Carter has written extensively on such subjects as the Navy of the Republic of Texas, the Spanish conquest of Mexico, the Aztec civilization. His work has been published in the magazines *Navy, Seapower, Naval Institute Proceedings, American Bar Association Journal,* the magazine *Houston,* the *Port of Houston Magazine,* the *Pelican,* the *Sunday Banner,* the *Military Engineer,* the magazine *The Shipyard Bulletin,* and elsewhere.

He is a member of the Bar, Supreme Court of Texas, and various Federal Courts in the United States, the Texas Bar Association, American Bar Association, and a number of clubs and societies.

1 / *Hidalgo's Dream*

This is the story of a lowly friar, who unknowingly swayed the destiny of four great nations. It is the story of how an obsession shaped history. It is the story of a righteous schemer. It is the story of Friar Francisco Hidalgo.

The story cannot begin until Hidalgo was about fifteen years of age, for no records exist of the early life of this humble Spanish friar. He was probably an orphan, and no one now knows either the date or place of his birth, or the names of his parents. He is said to have been fifteen years of age when he took the first vows of the Franciscan order, twenty-four when he first landed in Mexico, and sixty-seven when he died in 1726. This places the year of his birth as 1659, only a little more than a hundred and fifty years after Columbus discovered America.

Of average height and build, he was distinguished from his fellows only by his traits of character. He had the olive brown skin, black eyes, and black hair typical of many Spaniards. He wore the coarse gray robe and cowl used by the Franciscan missionary colleges in Mexico, and kept his hair and beard closely cropped. Not even his name is unusual, for Hidalgo is a common surname. He should not be confused with another Hidalgo — Miguel Hidalgo — also a priest, who lived a hundred years later and was one of the leaders in Mexico's struggle for independence from Spain.

A Franciscan historian describes Hidalgo as "a completely artless religious, and very zealous for the conversion of the Indians among whom he passed most of his life." He was filled "with abounding love, zeal, and had a personal magnetism that won many souls." His face "glowed with zeal." He always applied himself with a will to the duties given to him by his superiors, and his humble eloquence soon gained him a reputation as a successful missionary.

As we shall see, however, the foremost trait of his character — the quality that drove him through unbelievable hardships and disappointments — was a blind devotion to a dream, a vision, an obsession.

About 1682, when Hidalgo was only some twenty-three years old, the officials of the church and the Spanish government decided to place a missionary colegio or college of the Franciscan order in Mexico, then a part of the province called New Spain. The apostolic college was established in a Franciscan friary on the outskirts of the town of Querétaro, which lies in the mountains a hundred and thirty-five miles northwest of the capital, Mexico City.

Chosen to be one of the small band of friars to found the new colegio in the distant colony was the youthful Francisco Hidalgo. It must have been during the time he waited impatiently to leave for the fabled New World that his "vision" came to him in a dream, a dream so vivid and real that he never forgot even the smallest detail. In it he pictured himself standing in a wilderness setting, surrounded by a multitude of red-skinned savages, and preaching to them with fervor, pleading with them to become Christians.

At last the day came when the boyish friar, thrilled and full of enthusiasm, clambered aboard a top-heavy galleon and was actually on the way. As the crowded little ship lumbered through the long swells of the Atlantic, few of the gray-robed friars were as joyful as Hidalgo, however, and most of them were filled with dread. For, hundreds of lurid stories were current throughout the Spain of that day of the hordes of bloody pirates who infested the "Spanish Main," preying on the clumsy galleons.

If Hidalgo felt any fear, he dismissed it with a shrug of his shoulders, saying, "The Lord will protect me." With him, all else was drowned in the flood of his eagerness to get to New Spain and begin the labors of his dreams. He knew that it took months for the sluggish galleons to make the long voyage across the Atlantic Ocean and the Gulf of Mexico, but it seemed even longer to the impatient young friar. Mercifully, he could not know what awaited him and his companions when they landed in the Mexican port of Veracruz.

In the century that followed the conquests by the Spanish conquistadores of the vast reaches of the Americas, a growing stream of silver and gold flowed to Spain from its newly won colonies. Especially rich was the treasure from the great Aztec and Inca empires. Attracted by this wealth, the pirates in the Caribbean grew so bold and so numerous that at last they choked off most of the sea-borne commerce. Their special victims, of course, were the awkward Spanish ships as they returned home from Mexico or Panama laden with treasure.

Merchant ships sailing alone, even when they were armed, were no match for the pirate vessels; and in desperation the Spanish navy finally countered the corsairs by developing a convoy system. The plan was for the treasure ships to wait in port until a number of them were loaded and ready. Then they would all sail together, as a fleet and under the guard of escorting Spanish men-of-war.

Since the pirate ships worked singly and by themselves, the convoy device was effective in blocking them. In dismay they watched their intended victims sail safely through the seas that the pirates had formerly controlled with such success. Although the pirates were unruly and quarrelsome cutthroats who would not ordinarily work in harmony even with their own kind, the new situation quickly drove them to thoughts of working together.

About the time Hidalgo and his fellow friars sailed from Spain, therefore, a devils-convention met in Port Royal, the pirate stronghold on the island of Jamaica in the Caribbean Sea. Their purpose was to consider what they should do, and they quickly recognized that there was a promising remedy for their troubles. They could thwart the Spanish convoy system by getting at the treasure before it was entrusted to the convoys — while it still lay piled on the wharves in the seaports, awaiting shipment.

A raid on a protected seaport was far beyond the capability of any single ship or pirate crew, but the prize was rich enough to be worth even the cost of curbing their wild natures and working together in a common effort. So, at length, the assembled captains agreed to unite their ships in a loosely organized fleet which would be strong enough to attack the most promising victim — Veracruz.

Hidalgo and his companions knew nothing of all this, of course, as they looked forward to the end of their tedious journey. But Hidalgo's joy, and the thrill he felt at his first glimpse of the new world, soon turned to horror. For the stricken city now lay in ruins. The ashes of its sturdy buildings still smoked from the fires that had destroyed them. Its once busy streets were now deserted except for a few wretched survivors who were searching among the dead and dying for missing kinsmen.

Hidalgo's ship had barely missed arriving during the raid. A fleet of pirate ships had quickly silenced the cannon in the forts that guarded the harbor entrance, then sailed boldly into the helpless port. A savage horde of two thousand or more pirates swarmed ashore to sack the city. When at last they sailed away, they not only carried the gold and silver bars which had been piled high on the wharves, but also many of the people of the city — now destined for the slave market in Port Royal.

This, then, was the welcome that awaited the shocked and horrified Francisco Hidalgo and his fellow friars in the land that was to be their new home. Contrasting with the background of towering volcanoes and green tropical forests was the sickening scene of ravaged streets littered with dead bodies and groaning survivors.

Hurrying ashore, Hidalgo and his twenty-three companions set to work trying to help the wounded, console the dying, comfort the wounded and grief-stricken. Taking time only to tie a strip of cloth around his nose and mouth in a vain effort to shut out the stench of death, the young friar hurried from one victim to another. Doing what he could to help, he bandaged wounds, administered the last rites. Days passed without food or rest, but he kept on.

Despite the valiant work of the friars and the handful of able-bodied survivors, however, conditions in the city got worse. The meager supply of food quickly gave out. Not enough men were left alive to bury the dead. An epidemic seemed certain to follow, and finally the city officials ordered that the city be evacuated. So the friars had to stop their work in Veracruz, and resume their journey.

To go from Veracruz to Querétaro, where the new colegio was to be located, they now had to travel up the slopes of the great volcanoes and through the high mountain passes to Mexico City, then on over more mountains to their new home. It was a distance of more than a hundred and thirty leagues, or four hundred miles, on foot.

Walking two by two, the barefoot, robed friars attracted much attention as they plodded up the rough trails through the highlands. At every village along the way some of them stopped to preach and to minister to the natives. And the most eloquent of them all was the gentle but zealous Fray Francisco Hidalgo.

As soon as the new colegio was in operation on a solid basis, Hidalgo was put to work as a traveling missionary because of his skill in preaching. Despite his doubts, for he realized that he was unseasoned and still only twenty-four years old, the youthful friar was greatly pleased. His vision was still fresh in his mind. He was anxious to be about the task of carrying the Christian gospel to the hordes of naked savages who awaited him in the wilderness.

Getting ready for travel was simple for Hidalgo. He had no baggage to carry, no affairs to arrange. Living under a strict vow of poverty, his only possessions were the coarse gray robe and cowl with its rope-like cord around the waist, and the rosary beads and crucifix that dangled from the cord. In the friary he slept in a tiny cell that was furnished only with a hard bunk, one blanket, a rude chair and a shelf which served as a desk. On the road, however, he lay down and slept wherever night overtook him, many times with only his woolen habit to shield him from the chill of the desert wind. He ate what was given to him, or whatever small animals he might be able to catch along the road.

He usually traveled on foot, barefoot or wearing homemade sandals, although he sometimes enjoyed the luxury of a burro to ride. While he often journeyed alone, at times the friars worked in pairs or even with three in a group. On one such trip, he and two other friars traveled as far as Zacatecas, a hundred leagues, or three hundred miles, from Querétaro.

Here the missionaries so stirred the people of the town that they begged the visitors to stay with them and set up a new colegio in the nearby town of Guadalupe. This could not be done at the time, but later a colegio was established there.

Hidalgo stopped to preach to all who would come to hear him, even at the tiniest hamlet or isolated ranch, and success rewarded him everywhere. "Indecent costumes were abandoned, thefts and usuries were restored, ancient enmities reconciled, illicit and dishonest trade stopped; and above all, general confessions and public penitence were seen on every hand."

Notwithstanding his triumphs, even the sturdy body and dedicated mind of Hidalgo could not meet the demands of such a life. Finally, on one of his lengthy trips, after going without rest for twenty days, he fell sick. Irregular eating habits, long exposure to the biting cold of mountains and the searing heat of deserts had worn him down below the danger point. His illness failed to respond to the primitive treatment at hand in the countryside. Although he stubbornly tried to keep going, at last he had to give up and go back to the colegio to rest and be cured.

We can picture the unhappy young missionary, lying on the hard bunk in his cell, sick yet restless and chafing at the forced idleness. Yet it was not just lying there idle that made him restless and unhappy. For now, as he lay staring up at the dingy, smoke-grimed ceiling, he had to face the facts that for so long he had tried to ignore. The semi-civilized ranchers and villagers of central Mexico were not the wild Indians of his dreams. "I am not doing what God sent me to New Spain to do! I am not obeying my vision!"

Reproaching himself for such thoughts, he would try to put them out of his mind. "But it is a sin to be unhappy with my work! It is the work of the Lord. I have done what my superiors gave me to do. And I have done much good."

Still, no amount of such self-assurance could satisfy his conscience. The longer this inner debate went on, the more anxious he was to get to the work which he felt so strongly was God's will for him to do. He would ask — he would plead and beg — the "guardian" or superior of the colegio to send him on into the great unknown wilderness to the savages who needed him, and called out to him in his dreams.

2/A First Step

Better to understand the life and problems of young Francisco Hidalgo, it is helpful at this point to glance briefly at the Mexico and the New Spain of his day.

When the Aztec empire of Montezuma in the "Valley of Mexico" finally fell to Spain's invading army, it had to face up to the task of exploring the vast new domain lying north of it. Then came the dreary and even harder work of slowly and painfully pushing its rule and its religion across the rugged mountains and deserts — of building missions and forts and settlements in a far-away and often hostile country.

The region around Mexico City gave the Spanish little trouble. The people of the Aztec empire and some of those around its fringes were already highly civilized, and the harsh Montezuma and other rulers had imposed an orderly society on their subjects. Little more was needed except for Spain to station a few soldiers here and there, place Spaniards in the top government posts and Spanish priests, many of them members of the Franciscan Order, in the newly built churches. It was in the region lying farther north that the new Franciscan colegio was founded and in which Hidalgo had worked until now. But here too the countryside was then peopled by ranchers and farmers, not howling savages.

Although nearly two hundred years had passed since the discovery of the new land by Columbus, the Spanish occupation in the eastern part of Mexico still reached no farther to the north than the deserts that cover much of it. Only a few daring explorers and Franciscan and Jesuit missionaries had ventured into the vast territory that has since become the northeastern part of Mexico and the state of Texas.

Since their explorers had found no fabled cities of gold and no other treasure in that country, the Spaniards saw no reason to hurry settlers into it. Yet that was the "wilderness" in which Hidalgo had placed himself in his dreams. The wild, wandering tribes of Indians who lived in it were the people of his vision — the great harvest of souls that awaited him. And this is why he was troubled.

His pleas to the Father Guardian to send him into that great unknown land to the north must have been eloquent and persuasive, for they produced immediate results. As soon as he got his strength back, he and another friar set out on the rough trails and rutted roads that led toward the farthest Spanish outposts in the north. They not only had permission to continue their usual efforts in the role of traveling missionaries, but also to start missions if they found suitable locations for these.

Stopping to preach or to say Mass wherever they found people who would listen, the padres made slow progress. At last, however, they began to push into a parched and uninviting land. Yet even here, much to Hidalgo's delight, they sometimes drew crowds as large as those in central Mexico, and even more pleased to hear them. At last they reached the Villa de la Monclova, two hundred leagues — six hundred miles — from Querétaro. This was the last Spanish settlement. Everything farther on was "wilderness," except the missions in New Mexico which were staffed by friars from the Franciscan Province of the Holy Gospel, or Mexico City.

Hidalgo's eagerness to plunge into the unknown country

grew more acute. At last he was standing on the threshold of the land of the heathens, the "gentiles." There, under that horizon which he could now actually see, lived the naked, red-skinned savages of his vision and his dreams.

Nevertheless, his expectations soon suffered a chill. The Spanish commandant at Monclova first refused to help the missionaries in their work, saying that he could not spare any soldiers to guard a couple of wandering friars. Their urgent pleas failed to move him, and he not only rejected their requests, but finally forbade them from going any farther north — beyond the protection of the little garrison of soldiers in the settlement.

Hidalgo and his companion, Padre Estévez, faced a dilemma. Unwilling to accept defeat, to turn back, they did not know what to do. As they debated the question, and prayed for guidance, they kept on with their preaching in the plaza of the town. It was this dogged effort which at last led to a partial answer to their problem.

In the crowd that gathered in the plaza one day to listen to the friars were three half naked Indian braves. The savages understood a little Spanish, and they were fascinated by the gray-robed padres and their earnest pleas. After the service was over and the crowd had broken up, the Indians shyly sidled up to the missionaries, and there followed an exchange which must have been about like this:

One of the Indians, a tall, muscular brave, said to Padre Hidalgo, "Gray-robe, you speak good words."

Although the man spoke in a mixture of his native dialect and Spanish, Hidalgo understood him, and was pleased. "Thank you, my son," he replied.

"Will you speak your words to my people?"

"Your people? Where are your people?"

"The place that the white men call Boca de Leones."

"How far away is it?"

"Two — three day walk," he held up three fingers.

"And you want to take us there? To talk to your people?"

"Yes, gray-robe."

Fray Hidalgo shook his head. "The capitán will not let us go any farther north, my son," he said sadly, pointing to the horizon. "We cannot go with you."

"But it is not north, gray-robe," the brave said.

"Not north? Then which way is it?" Hidalgo asked, his voice once more eager.

"Toward the sun of mid-morning," the Indian replied, pointing in that direction.

"Ah! Southeast!" the young friar turned to his companion, and with a sly wink, said, "The capitán only mentioned north, you remember?"

"Sí! It is true, brother."

"This may be the answer to our prayers!"

"I agree! Indeed it is."

Suddenly hopeful once more, Hidalgo turned back to the Indian and asked, "How big is your tribe? Are there many people?"

"Many."

"And you think they will listen to us?"

"You come, gray-robe. They will listen."

Hidalgo looked back at his companion once more. Friar Estévez nodded his head in answer to the question that it was not necessary to put into words, and Hidalgo faced the Indian to say, "We will go, my son. When can you leave?"

"When the sun rises tomorrow."

"Very well. We will be ready."

After a three day walk, the two padres and their three Indian guides reached Boca de Leones, now the site of the Mexican town of Villaldama. The friars liked what they saw, and agreed that it seemed to be a good place for a mission. The soil appeared to be fertile. A small river not only carried enough water for a mission, but even promised to be ample to irrigate a field of beans and corn for the food supply. So Hidalgo told the three guides, "If enough people come to join us, we will build a mission here."

"We will bring them in," the savages assured them.

With a little help from the Indians, the missionaries set to work building a chapel. It was a mere frame of light tree limbs over which they could put a straw thatching for a roof and sides of sticks and mud, but it would serve as a chapel until a better one could be built. Naming it San Pedro de Boca de Leones, they began their ministry. The "gentiles" did not crowd in as they had hoped, but at length enough converts were assembled for Padre Hidalgo to start a regular teaching schedule for them.

Despite this slow start, young Hidalgo was much happier here at Boca de Leones. This arid land was not exactly the lush wilderness he had visualized, and the handful of savages that he baptized was not the multitude of his dreams. But at least it was more like it than central Mexico had been. His superiors back in the colegio were pleased, too, and although the cactus-studded area was not thickly populated, they soon sent another missionary to found an additional mission about halfway between Boca de Leones and Monclova.

Nevertheless, Padre Hidalgo was not destined to stay at San Pedro de Boca de Leones very long. One day an Indian brought in a peculiar looking rock from the nearby mountains — a dense and heavy rock. This proved to be silver ore, and a mining camp quickly sprang up near the little mission. A settlement soon followed, and within a year it grew into a thriving mining town. Before two years passed the town was large enough and stable enough for the mission to be given a more regular and permanent status.

Thus Padre Hidalgo lost his first mission post due to the evolution of the mission itself. He was crushed to have to leave, but he patiently bowed to what he thought must be the will of God. With a heavy heart he left to go back to the colegio and resume the work of an evangelist in the more settled area of central Mexico.

But like the coyote pup after his first taste of blood, Hidalgo would never again be content with anything except the frontier. No longer did he depend on some vague dream — he had felt the soul satisfying thrill of really working among flesh and blood savages. In his heart he knew that he would return to this work of his vision in God's own time.

3 / A Fateful Shipwreck

During the years that the still young Hidalgo spent in central Mexico and at Boca de Leones, important events were taking place elsewhere in the world. Many of them made kings and princes tremble in far off Europe. Some of them would completely alter the course of his own life. Let us now leave him trudging the rocky, mountain trails around Querétaro, while we look at these things that, unknown to him, were shaping history.

About the time Hidalgo first came to New Spain, a French adventurer explored the Mississippi River. This man is called La Salle in the history books of the United States. Floating down the mighty stream from the Great Lakes to its mouth, he was deeply impressed by the fertile land that bounded it, and decided to begin to colonize it at once.

Planning to begin with a settlement near the mouth of the great river, he hurried back to Canada and then on to France. There he set about getting money and settlers for the project. Some two years later, he sailed from the home country with four ships carrying about four hundred colonists, and headed for the Gulf of Mexico and the mouth of the Mississippi.

Bad luck and trouble beset the little squadron from the start. A series of storms and foul weather plagued it. Then, near the island of Santo Domingo, a Spanish warship attacked it, capturing one of the four ships. The three remaining vessels finally reached the Gulf of Mexico after many delays. Navigating there in unknown currents and with the crude instruments of that day, they missed their goal.

La Salle thought that he was east of the river's mouth, although in fact he was far to its west. Acting on this belief, he turned the ships to run on a westerly course along the low, swampy coast, searching for the Mississippi. At length he sighted the entrance to what is now called Matagorda Bay, on the central Texas coast, and thinking this might be the place he sought, he decided to enter it and find out.

While leading the column of vessels in, the flagship ran hard aground on a sand bar near the mouth of the bay. All efforts to free her failed, and La Salle had to abandon her, transferring all the passengers to another ship. At this point, the captain of the third ship refused to risk his craft in the treacherous channel. Instead of following La Salle into the bay, he turned away, and later returned to France. On board the one remaining ship, La Salle cautiously felt his way over the sand bar, and succeeded in getting into the bay.

Once inside, he soon saw that this was not the mouth of the mighty river he sought. He still felt that he was not far from it, however, so he decided that the further search could be carried out more easily over the land than by sailing along the dangerous coast. So, the colonists from the anchored flagship and those from the wrecked vessel which still lay on the bar, went ashore.

Using planks from the wreck, the French built temporary shelters and a fort. La Salle named this Fort Saint Louis, in honor of his king, Louis XIV, and using it as a base, began the search by land in all directions. He and his men never found the Mississippi, and eventually death overtook most of them, either in the hostile wilderness or the feeble little fortress.

News traveled slowly in those days, and it was months later that rumors began to reach Spanish ears that the hated French had put a colony on the Texas coast — Spanish territory. These rumors created great excitement and dismay both in Madrid and in Mexico City, and in the four years that followed, the Spanish sent out five different squadrons of warships to search for the intruders. Although the searchers sailed along the entire coast line from Mexico to Florida, no sign of the French was ever sighted from the sea.

Meanwhile other parties of Spaniards hunted on the land side, but they too failed to find any invaders. Finally, a report reached Governor Alonso de León of a white man who was living with the Indians somewhere north of the Río Grande. Thinking that this might be a clue to the French, the governor led a small troop of soldiers across the river and into what is now Texas. Their search did result in finding a white man who said his name was Jean Géry, and who claimed to know all about La Salle and his colony.

Although it was soon apparent that the mind of the white stranger was addled, this was the best lead yet, so the governor reported it to the viceroy in Mexico City at once. This, of course, intensified the near-hysteria about a French incursion into the territory of New Spain.

Eventually the crumbling remains of Fort Saint Louis were found on the shores of what is today called Matagorda Bay. But its worm-eaten ramparts were now manned only by the few whitened bones left by the Indians who had overwhelmed the little garrison. What is important to our story is that this French misadventure spurred the Spanish to send out search parties that ranged over great distances, Thus they became familiar with a great deal of territory that had been unexplored before and in which they had not previously been interested.

It also led to another incident of importance, the chance encounter by Governor Alonso's men with an Indian buffalo hunter. This man said that he was a chief of one of the Tejas tribes whose home was far to the northeast. This was an area that was not only unexplored, but that lay along the frontier with the French domain of Louisiana.

His home country, the Tejas chief said, was covered with thick forests and dotted with many Indian villages. He was unable to tell the governor very much about the French, but he did seem to know a little about the Christian religion, and begged Alonso to send missionaries to his land and people.

All these factors combined to focus attention on what is today northeast Texas, and its unmarked, nebulous boundary with French Louisiana. Governor Don Alonso de León was therefore authorized not only to explore and to search for evidence of French invasion, but also to place missions in the region. Thus the Spanish hoped to block any French attempt to expand their rule into New Spain in the future, and with this end in view, Alonso's party included four Franciscan friars, headed by a venerable missionary named Damián Massanet.

Although they groped deep into the dense pine forests that covered the rolling hills of the land of the Tejas, the Spanish scouting squads failed to find any trace of the French. But they did explore and learn much about the new country.

Of even more importance, a site was selected for a mission. It lay "on the bank of a small creek of good water," the San Pedro Creek, some seven miles from the Neches River, and near the present-day town of Weches in Houston County, Texas. The name given the new mission was San Francisco de los Tejas, and the date of its establishment was May 24, 1690. A commemorative park now marks the spot where it stood.

With a little help from the Indians of a nearby village of the Nabedache tribe, a branch of the Tejas nation, the Spaniards put up a brush arbor to use as a chapel until a more substantial church and other buildings could be built. Then, leaving the other three friars and three soldiers to continue the work while they went for help, Governor Alonso and Friar Massanet set out with the rest of the expedition on the return journey to Mexico.

Friar Massenet visualized the erection of a whole chain of missions in eastern Texas. He actually did receive the approval of the viceroy to his plan. But more was needed than mere approval. First he had to get the supplies needed for the venture, then assemble them and arrange for carrying them on the long journey. He also had to recruit manpower, and this is where Friar Francisco Hidalgo enters the picture.

As to Governor Alonso de León, when he returned from the expedition into eastern Texas, he was greeted with the news that he was being replaced as the governor of Coahuila by Domingo Terán de los Rios. This governor proved to be a man of considerable vigor, but he was new in the post, and hesitant about such a formidable project. Nor did he know how to grope through the maze of government red tape involved.

It is worthy of note that the title of the post to which Terán was appointed, "Governor of Coahuila" up to that time, was now "Governor of Coahuila and Texas." This is the first official use of the name Texas, and thus Domingo Terán de los Rios became the first man to bear the title of governor of Texas.

It is easy for us, two hundred and fifty years later, to pick out the mistakes made by the Spanish in their almost frantic efforts to counter the supposed threat by the French to settle in Texas. The site where the new Mission San Francisco de los Tejas was founded was six hundred miles from the nearest Spanish outpost at Monclova. Yet little or no thought was given to the support or protection of the mission. A long leap of six hundred miles across an unsettled and unknown wilderness was foolhardy, of course, but even worse was the failure to provide some means to sustain it. They seem to have taken for granted that the Indians would be friendly, and that the isolated mission could and would feed and sustain itself without outside help.

It is significant, too, that the emphasis was on a mission rather than a military outpost, although one of the main purposes was to protect New Spain from the French. The Spaniards had used the mission system with success among the Indians of Mexico, so no doubt it was natural for them to try the same thing even among the far-away tribes of the Tejas nation. But failing to take into account that the people and the conditions were so wholly different in the two areas would prove to be a fatal mistake.

4/A Dream Comes True

Although Fray Hidalgo had known of the expeditions sent out to hunt the French and to found a mission in East Texas — these expeditions were called entradas, entrances — he had not accompanied them, no doubt to his great disappointment. So, when the governor and Friar Massanet returned with plans to build a chain of missions among the Tejas, we can be sure that Hidalgo asked to be sent there. In fact, we can safely guess that he did more than merely ask for the assignment. He surely used all the influence he could command, and all the eloquence for which he was noted, to get it.

Whatever the means he employed, they succeeded. In due time he received orders from his superiors to join Padre Massanet and the group that was gathering north of Monclova, preparing to march to the land of the Tejas. It must have been a joyful day for him when at last he set out over the sun-baked trail.

When he arrived at the meeting place, he found that most of the people who were to go had already arrived. Nine Franciscan priests and three brothers were in the party, headed by the gaunt and aging Padre Massanet, the most senior of them. In command of the entrada as a whole was the new governor, Domingo Terán de los Rios.

Fifty mounted troopers formed the escort, looking very

handsome in their red and green and white uniforms and peaked leather caps, their lances glinting in the sun and their horses prancing. The supply train comprised a dozen or so pack mules and three crude, two-wheeled carts pulled by teams of oxen. In addition there was a mixed herd of cattle, sheep, and goats, plus twenty extra horses.

It was now the latter part of May, 1691, and a scorching sun bore down in full force as the column snaked across the cactus-dotted country toward the Río Grande. But Padre Hidalgo was happy. At last he was really on his way to the land of his vision! All this must have seemed to be a promising start for the venture, but the entrada was plagued by trouble from the beginning.

Reaching the Río Grande, the marchers were surprised to find it in flood. It usually rose and overflowed in the winter and early spring, but now, in June, it was a "gunshot in width." A trooper rode into the swirling current to test its depth, but had to turn back as the water quickly rose to the level of his horse's back. Terán ordered a halt, and the party made camp while scouts searched up and down the river to see if there was a better place to cross.

Any delay was galling to Hidalgo, but making the best of things, he joined his companions in a dinner of cold, rubbery tortillas, baked beans, and strong goat's milk cheese. Then, as darkness settled over the valley, he picked out a spot under a drooping willow tree and lay down to sleep. About midnight, however, he woke with a start. A sudden uproar filled the camp — shouts and what he at first thought was thunder. The ground began to shake as though an earthquake had struck. Hidalgo jumped to his feet. At first he thought it was a tempest, but as his mind cleared, he realized that the horses had stampeded. Something had panicked them — perhaps wolves, perhaps prowling Indians.

To hunt in the dark was futile, but as soon as daylight came, everyone — friars, soldiers, and all — joined in trying to find the horses and round them up. They had run a long way in their panic, however, and then wandered off in all directions in a random hunt for grass. Even though the roundup went on all day, only a few more than a third of the missing horses were brought in. After three days half of them were still missing. Not even enough had been found to mount all of the cavalrymen.

The river continued to rise, too, making the crossing more dangerous with each passing hour. The water was already much too deep for the sheep and goats, and even for the oxen. Nor was there any wood for building rafts, as the only trees in the region were small willows along the stream and some stunted mesquite trees scattered over the parched countryside.

The only way to get the small animals and supplies across was to carry them on the backs of swimming horses. The soldiers set to work, swimming back and forth across the racing stream, carrying a sheep or a goat or a load of supplies on their backs or in their arms. Trip after trip, back and forth, the horses swam through the swirling current. Three more horses were lost — drowned during the perilous swim.

The carts and heavier supplies had to be left behind, and when at last the task was finished, horses and men alike fell to the ground, exhausted. Still, they were on the Texas side at last, and thankful for it. The dry bed of a creek seemed to offer a soft place where weary bodies could rest, so they made camp there, piling the precious supplies nearby.

We can imagine Hidalgo and his fellows, their wet gray robes clinging to them, as they knelt to give thanks that the crossing was finally finished. They were also thankful that it was summer, and hoped that the coarse robes would dry

Reconstruction of the first Mission of San Francisco de los Tejas in the Texas State Park near Weches. Founded in 1690, this mission was the scene of Father Francisco Hidalgo's first missionary efforts in east Texas from 1691 to 1693.

MAP SHOWING LOCATION OF FIRST MISSION IN EASTERN TEXAS, AND ITS RELATION TO FRENCH TERRITORY AS WELL AS TO THE FORT BUILT BY THE STRANDED FRENCH EXPLORER LA SALLE.

Scale: ½" equals 80 mi. (32 leagues).

out before the chill of the desert night moved in. Gulping down a few bites of cold, soggy food, they lay down in the sand to sleep.

Their troubles were still not over, however, for in the middle of their first night in Texas a sudden thunderstorm swept down the river valley. Awakened by a sudden flash of lightning, Hidalgo jumped to his feet to the accompaniment of a loud clap of thunder. In a moment another flash of lightning lit up the scene, and he saw a trickle of water in the dry sand of the creek bed. Knowing how fast such a trickle can grow into a muddy torrent, he ran to the bank. Yelling a warning to his companions, he began to scramble up the brush-choked slope. As he reached the top, drenched to the skin from rain, he looked back and saw that he had barely escaped being swept off his feet by a roaring flood that had already built up behind him.

All of the men survived, but most of the supplies that had been ferried across the river with so much labor and peril were washed down the creek in the flood, and lost. And as a final blow, the horses had stampeded again. Stunned by the chain of tragedies, Padre Hidalgo voiced the bitter conviction that "The infernal furies instigated the storm! Satan is trying to stop us!"

The other friars agreed, "Sí, sí! El Diablo fears that we will convert all the savages to Christianity!"

"We will sing a High Mass to crush his evil plans!" Friar Massanet ordered. "As soon as morning comes."

When at last the weakened little expedition resumed its march, it crept slowly northeastward for about ten days without further setbacks. Gradually the arid, brush-covered country changed to a broken land of many streams whose limestone banks were dotted with pecan and walnut trees. Big patches of grass began to appear here and there.

Soon Fray Hidalgo saw his first buffalo — "an animal that at first sight is beautiful, but on closer observation is ugly. It is larger than an ox, with hoofs very much the same; and the horns, although very black, are much shorter and curved. The buffalo neck up to the forehead is ill shaped. The bison has long hair which obstructs its view. For that reason it runs against the wind. The animal is very malodorous, does not hear well, and sees less on account of the mane of hair. It has a tail like a hog. It runs very fast, and a horse must be very quick to catch it. The bison has more meat than two steers, and is very wholesome and good. Some of the men ate too much meat and had stomach ache."

On June 13th, crossing a "fine country with broad plains, the most beautiful in New Spain," the governor says in his diary, "we camped on the banks of an arroyo (now named the San Antonio River), adorned by a great number of trees, cedars, willows, cypresses, osiers, oaks, and many other kinds. This I called San Antonio de Padua, because we reached it on his day." Friar Massanet adds that there were "a great many fish, and upon the highlands a great number of wild chickens."

An Indian village stood near some springs of clear, sweet water. This place, later the site of Mission San Juan Capistrano, and within the present city of San Antonio, Texas, was called Yanaguana by the Indians (Refreshing Waters). Although he could not foresee it, of course, Fray Hidalgo would return to this spot many times in the future.

Since the following day was Corpus Christi day, the company rested, celebrating the occasion with a High Mass, gun salutes and ceremonies, much to the delight of the Indians. On the 15th, after passing out beads, tobacco, rosaries, and other gifts to the natives, the column moved out once more, heading in an easterly direction "over level lands without woods," now occupied by the Brooks Air Force Base.

Making twelve to fifteen miles a day, the creeping entrada finally reached the Trinity River. Here a messenger met them with news from the fledgling mission in the piney woods ahead. And the news was bad. One of the three missionaries left there by Governor Alonso had died in an epidemic of fever which swept through the country, killing some three thousand of the Tejas. The other missionaries and the soldiers were on the verge of starvation.

Hurrying ahead over the rolling, red clay hills and through thick forests, Hidalgo finally caught a glimpse through the pines of his new home. It was all just as he had seen it in his vision. This was no arid waste, no sandy desert where only cactus and greasewood grew. It was a fertile land of tall, straight trees. It was the land of his dreams!

Stumps still dotted the clearing, for the pitiful handful of men left there by Alonso and Massanet, had not been able to do much. As yet the clearing was only about two hundred paces square, far too small to include fields or pastures. But at least a start had been made, and beyond the clearing, Hidalgo could see San Pedro Creek which promised ample water for the needs of the new mission.

Amid the stumps and the piles of brush a joyful reunion took place, with a dozen half-naked Indian braves standing nearby, aloof but curious as they watched the antics of the happy whiteskins. And Hidalgo must have breathed a deep sigh of satisfaction as he took in the scene. At last, after all those years! Eight of them had passed since that day in Veracruz when he first set foot on the soil of New Spain. Now, for the first time, he felt truly satisfied deep within his soul. Surely, this was his destiny!

The next morning, after a Mass of thanksgiving, Don Domingo and the troopers who had horses rode off to explore the country to the north and east, and to search once more for signs of the French. As they disappeared into the forest, the friars and soldiers who were left behind set to work with a feeling of urgency. Summer was now far advanced. Already some of the leaves on the oaks and gums were tinged with the yellows and reds of autumn. The chapel and cabins must be made ready and more huts built for the winter.

The missionaries had hoped for help from the Indians, but this proved to be a vain hope. It had been hard enough to get the natives in Mexico to work, but these were even worse. Many of them came to the mission, but only to watch in wonder as the white men labored. "They were interested only in hunting and fishing, and in stealing."

Long before the building and preparing for winter was finished, all of the soldiers and even some of the friars were discouraged. Already some of them were ready to give up, to let the French have the country if they wanted it. But not Hidalgo. And not the faithful old Father Massanet.

Now the leaves began to change color faster, and some to drop from the trees. Frost lay on the stumps and the sparse grass each morning. Soon the first "norther" hit, bringing a blast of chilled air from the great plains to the north and west. The blustery north wind cut through Hidalgo's heavy gray robe and cowl as though they were made of cheesecloth.

By the time Don Domingo got back from his scouting trip, all but five of the missionaries were ready to leave the project and go back with him to Mexico. Only the austere and inspired Hidalgo, the dedicated Massanet, and three others were even willing to stay, much less to think of building a whole chain of missions. Governor Terán left a squad of soldiers to guard the five friars, and with the others, started the return to Mexico in January of 1692. As he rode away into the forest, even Fray Hidalgo must have felt some foreboding of disaster. Even he had to admit to himself that the odds were very heavy indeed against the success of the lonely outpost mission.

Neither he nor the staunch Massenet dared to put their feelings into words, however. Instead, they worked harder to finish the cabins, gather enough firewood to last through the winter, and make the few other preparations that were within their power.

5 / *Hidalgo's Vow*

It was plain to the Indians of the vicinity that not enough soldiers had been left at the lonely little mission to guard the supplies, cattle, sheep, and goats. The animals lacked pastures, too, and had to scatter through the forest to browse on twigs of trees and scattered tufts of grass. It was easy to shoot and eat, or steal and drive away, such animals. Those spared by the Indians grew weak and bony from a lack of proper food, and thus became easy prey for the bitter cold and disease.

Few of the Indians became converts, and even fewer of them would help to clear fields for crops of corn and beans. Only one elderly chief, his family, and some two dozen other natives could be persuaded to settle near the mission — to become Christians and "Mission Indians."

To make things worse, some disease broke out among the small group who had built their hogans near the mission. It was not a serious sickness, but it quickly spread to their wild brethren in the forest, and soon grew into an epidemic. A rumor started among the savages that this sickness was caused by the holy water which the friars used to baptize converts. More than half of those at the mission deserted and fled into the wilderness, to resume their wild life once more. Only the old chief, Totonac, his family, and a handful of others stayed on at Mission San Francisco de los Tejas.

Taking advantage of all this, an ambitious young chief, called Bernardino by the Spanish, stirred up the Indians even more. Their hostility grew into a threat of an actual attack. Warned of this by their converts, and fearing a massacre, the Spaniards finally had to station a soldier at a loaded cannon, ready to touch a match to the fuse if a sudden assault struck the mission.

Long before spring came, most of the food supply was used up, or stolen. The store dropped below the danger level, and rationing had to be started. Even so, the dole had to be lowered several times to stretch the supply out as much as it could be. By adding rabbits and field mice trapped in the forest, and an occasional gift of venison by Totonac, the little garrison somehow survived until spring came with its wild berries and herbs. A small patch of corn and beans yielded a harvest of only a month's supply. An appeal for help resulted in a few supplies from Mexico, but the amount was far from enough to last through another winter. Two more of the discouraged friars went back to Mexico with the supply train, leaving only three missionaries and half a dozen soldiers.

This was the situation when once more the green in the leaves of the hardwoods began to change to autumn's yellows and reds. Something had to be done, and soon. Friar Massanet called the little group together for a meeting in the tiny log chapel. In fancy we can see the grim-faced old friar standing before his fellows, his coarse gray robe hanging loose from his bony shoulders. Solemnly he recited what they already knew so well — another winter was bearing down, they had no food to carry them through it, not only had their efforts to convert the Indians failed, but an attack might come at any time. No sensible course was left but to abandon the mission.

Every head nodded approval — except that of Padre Hidalgo. It was his nature to jump to his feet and protest, "I do not admit that we have failed! We have not! God is testing our faith! We would be yielding to Satan if we gave up the fight. Do not desert our mission and our work, my brothers. Do not abandon God's work here!"

No one agreed. Only a sad dissent showed on the weather-beaten faces of those who looked up from the crude benches. No sympathy lit up their eyes. But a defiant Hidalgo went on, his voice shaking with emotion, "I see that you are determined. But I cannot go. I shall stay, whatever the rest may do. I am not afraid to face yon Indians alone. God will protect me! Else he will let me join the host of blessed martyrs who have bled for the Holy Cross." Sinking to the rough bench, he buried his face in his hands.

Padre Massanet hesitated only a moment. His voice at once both gentle but firm, he said, "I'm sorry, Hidalgo, but we must go. And today! We'll carry what food and weapons we can, and the vestments and holy vessels from the altar. All else must be set afire. What will not burn, we'll bury so nothing will be left for the pagans or the French. Now go — all of you! And hurry!"

The other men quickly got to their feet and hurried out. Hidalgo still sat with his face cupped in his hands. Fray Massanet walked slowly over to him and placing a gentle hand on his head said, "Arise, my son. We must gather the sacred vessels for the journey."

"No, good father. I'll stay here. It is the work that God ordered me to do!"

"You cannot stay here alone, Hidalgo! It would serve no good purpose. To be a martyr is a blessed death, but only when something is gained by it — only if it achieves some goal. Our duty is to go back to Mexico and persuade the governor or the viceroy to give us more soldiers, and tools and supplies, so the mission can be rebuilt and then survive."

"God should strike me dead if I leave. I cannot go!"

"Then I'll have to tell the soldiers to bind you and carry you."

Hidalgo looked up into the older man's eyes, and saw that he meant what he said. In a voice that was no more than a whisper he replied, "To carry me would only make your escape harder — slower."

"Sí. But I'll not leave you here alone," Massanet said firmly.

Further protest was futile. Hidalgo stood up and faced Massanet. "Do you really think that we can persuade them — the viceroy — to send us back again, good father?"

"We can try, my son. We can try."

Hidalgo hesitated for a moment, then said, "Very well, good father. I must not be a burden. I'll go. But only so I can return." He turned and walked toward the altar to begin the packing.

When the friars came out of the chapel a few minutes later, each carrying a bundle, Hidalgo saw that the eager soldiers had lost no time in getting ready for the retreat. A small pile of packs and parcels lay ready on the ground near the chapel. He put his own bundle on the pile. Then he looked up and saw a group of Indians standing in front of their hogans near the edge of the clearing — Totonac and his little band of converts.

Aging but still tall and erect, the chief stood with his arms folded across his waist. Like a stolid bronze statue he watched the Spaniards as they got ready to leave. Touched by the sight, Fray Hidalgo turned to Padre Massanet and said, "I must bid Totonac farewell."

"Very well," Friar Massanet replied. "But do not tarry

long. We must leave at once."

Hidalgo hurried across the clearing toward the small knot of redskins. As he neared them, the solemn, dignified chief continued to watch with an indifferent air which Hidalgo knew was only a mask to hide his true feelings. The friar hesitated for a moment, suddenly unable to find words. Finally he blurted out awkwardly in the mixture of Indian dialect and Spanish that both of them understood, "Totonac, the whiteskins are leaving."

"My eyes have told me so. Why you leave?"

"We have no food for the winter. We do not even have candles to burn on the altar."

"Has Totonac angered his whiteskin friends?"

"No, no! Totonac has been a faithful friend. So have these others here with you. But you are so few!" Despite his effort to suppress it, Hidalgo knew that his voice must carry a note of bitterness.

Totonac drew himself up, and seemed even taller as he replied. "You know, father, that all Indians are not the same. Bernardino is evil. His braves are evil. But we are your friends."

"I know that well, Totonac."

"If you want a bigger hogan, we'll build it for you. We'll go to church when you ring the bell. We'll bring you venison when we hunt. We'll bring fish when we fish."

"God bless you, my son. I do not want to leave. Please believe me. But the other whiteskins will it. They will not let me stay here alone."

The Indian did not reply with words, but when he turned his shining black eyes on Hidalgo, the hurt in them was plain. After a long pause, he asked, "Gray-robe father come back?"

Padre Hidalgo turned away to hide his face. He looked

across the clearing at the tiny log chapel and the hastily built cabins. Already smoke seeped through the cracks between the logs, while here and there bright orange flames leaped up from the thatched roofs. Crude though they were, Hidalgo had been proud of those rough cabins. He remembered well how many aching muscles they had cost him, how many hundreds of blisters. In them I have spent many hours of sadness, and many of triumph, he thought. In that chapel I have sent up many prayers for my redskin children.

He clenched his fists and turned back to face the old chief with all the self-control he could summon up. "Totonac, I'm sorry. I cannot sway my brethren. But I give you my word — I promise —" he lifted the crucifix that hung from his neck and held it out, "I swear by this Holy Cross, that I shall return. Some day, I'll return! I go to plead with my chiefs to send me back with more men and supplies. But my thoughts — my heart — my prayers — will be here with you, always."

So it came to pass that Fray Hidalgo and his fellow Spaniards began the long tramp back to Mexico. "Stalked by the savages, they trudged back through the wilderness which they had entered with such high hopes two years before."

Four months passed on the trail. It was early in the year 1694, therefore, before the refugees reached Monclova, where they once more enjoyed the luxury of being safe and full of food. The three footsore friars rested here for a few days to regain their strength before continuing on toward the colegio in Querétaro. Finally back "at home" in the colegio, many weeks later, Hidalgo was dismayed when his pleas for supplies for a return to Texas were curtly refused. Not a single doubloon could he get from the Franciscans, nor from any other source.

In fact, the history of the colegio tells us that in those days the name "Tejas" was so hated that no one dared to utter it. Thus the grieving Hidalgo was even denied the small comfort of talking to his companions about his longing to go back. Nevertheless, his resolve remained strong, even though locked in his own breast. He could only hope and pray — and wait. And through it all his abiding faith never weakened, never faltered. Somehow, sometime, he would go back. Although unhappy and frustrated, he could console himself with the thought that he was still young — only in his thirties. There was time.

The reaction to the failure in Texas was so strong, and both friars and all other Spaniards were so bitter, that no one cared to analyze or even think about the reasons for it. No trace of French invasion had been found except the pitiful little Fort Saint Louis, garrisoned only by the bones of its builders. The threat from France seemed to have receded. It was easy now to ignore or forget.

Texas was very, very far away from Mexico City, where the viceroy and other high officials of New Spain lived. It was even farther from Madrid. No gold, no treasure, had been found north of the Río Grande. Even if Spain had felt an urge to colonize, it could not furnish enough Spaniards to settle in all the world-wide empire it claimed. And Texas did not seem as important as many other places.

Moreover, Spain was not as strong as it had once been. In the two hundred years since the discoveries by Columbus, the fabulous treasures of Peru and Mexico had been squandered in fruitless adventures. The energy and drive of the conquistadores — the early conquerers — had faded. Both the vigor and the wealth of Spain had been drained into the quicksand of European politics and intrigues. None was left for a distant and wild and unknown frontier province.

The mission system devised by the Spanish had three aims — to convert the Indians to Christianity, to teach them European morals and customs, and to hold the land for the Spanish crown. The Mission San Francisco de los Tejas did none of these things. While it is true that the French did not attempt to send settlers into east Texas, their failure to do so was not due to a fear of the Spanish, but rather to the fact that they were interested only in trade with the Indians. They had no wish to settle the vast reaches west of the Mississippi River.

Notwithstanding its failure, however, the abandoned east Texas project had some value for the Spanish. Much had been learned about the geography of the distant frontier region, and about the natives there. It was now clearer to them that while the mission system had succeeded well in Mexico among a people who lived in a farming and herding culture, many changes had to be made to adapt it to the nomadic hunting and fishing tribes of Texas.

Finally, the Spaniards were beginning to realize that such an outpost as Mission San Francisco de los Tejas could succeed only if it was fully supported until it became self-sustaining. It could not "live off the country around it." And besides the mere matter of food, a fatal weakness was a lack of "stepping-stones" — a chain of missions and forts to support and reinforce the outpost. Strong points were needed to back up the front line. This lesson would be valuable in the future, not only in Texas, but also in Arizona and in California, where Padre Junípero Serra and his colleagues would be careful to space their missions only a day's journey apart.

6 / The Road Back

The three years that followed Hidalgo's return from Texas must have seemed like centuries to him. His new assignment was the same sort of traveling missionary work in central Mexico that he had done during the years after he first came to New Spain. He stuck to the work that was given him with a dogged determination, and tried to be patient. Memories of his vision and of his still unhonored promise to the old Indian burned within him, however. His heart was sick and his nights troubled. Only the firm belief sustained him that sooner or later a way to realize his dreams would open up.

Then one day a new director, or "guardian" arrived at the colegio. And to Hidalgo's great joy, the new official was an old friend of his, Padre Antonio Margil de Jesús. Padre Margil had been one of the original group of twenty-four friars who founded the colegio, but he had been on duty in what is now Central America for about thirteen years.

It was not only seeing an old friend and fellow worker that pleased Hidalgo, for he also saw that the appoinment of Margil might be favorable to his own secret designs. He felt sure that this old friend would at least listen to him with sympathy and interest, and he also believed that Margil would be more inclined to agree with him. For Margil had been gone for so many years, far away from the bitter failure of the Tejas mission, that his mind was not poisoned by the defeatism and apathy so prevalent in Mexico.

Hidalgo went to work on Padre Margil as quickly as he could and with all his ability to persuade. As he had hoped, the new director not only had an open mind, but also shared Hidalgo's anxiety about the savages in the unknown lands to the north. Both of them realized that it would be too much to hope for that Mission San Francisco de los Tejas could be restored at once, so Fray Margil wrote to the viceroy in vague terms about the need for missions "in the north."

Months of waiting followed the sending of the letter, but Hidalgo expected delays. The letter slowly worked its way through the red tape and tiresome routine of the viceroy's office and staff. Eight months passed but when finally a reply did come, it was favorable. The viceroy wrote that "Having news of the copious harvest of pagan souls in the north, who are without the light of the Gospel," he approved the plan to found a new mission in the region beyond Monclova, and later, perhaps others. The letter went on to say that the viceroy was ordering the governor to choose a suitable site for a new mission, and to help the friars in their project.

Hidalgo was jubilant. At last he could return to work among the wild "gentiles." This was not going back to the Tejas, but at least it was a step — a very long step — along the road. He wasted no time in getting started. With a fellow friar named Salazar as a companion, he left at once on the tiring journey over the mountains and near-desert to Monclova, two hundred and fifty leagues away.

When they got to Monclova, the governor gave them an escort of troopers under the command of a Capitán Tobar, and also named this officer as his representative to carry out all the official duties needed for the project. The party set out, and after first inspecting several sites which the Indians told them about, they came to a spot called El Ojo de Agua de Lampazos, of Lampasos Springs. This lay about fifty miles east of Monclova, and forty miles north of the mining town at Boca de Leones where Hidalgo had built a mission ten years before.

Here the party found a small tribal village of Indians, a few of whom had spent a little time at one of the missions nearer to Monclova. The springs of water promised a steady supply of water for a mission, and even enough for irrigating its fields and pastures, and there were enough Indians within easy reach of the site to justify a mission.

Even more persuasive, however, was the exciting story the Indians told. One dark night a few days before the Spaniards came, the Indians said, they had seen an unearthly show which they were sure was a sign sent by the Great Spirit. "The sky suddenly lit up with fifty spheres of light, which seemed as stars loosed from their moorings." These grew brighter and streaked across the heavens "like charged tongues of descending fire." Awed by the story, the friars reverently agreed that this must indeed be a divine mandate to place a mission here. So they set to work at once.

Once the exact location for the mission was settled, actual building began. The history of the colegio describes it in these words: "A chapel of straw was begun on November 23, the holy day of San Diego de Alcalá. The participants, all barefooted, marched in solemn procession to the new hermitage, holding high a wooden cross as a royal banner of redemption. They sang a hymn and celebrated the Mass of the saint, giving thanks to the Lord for the new harvest of souls."

Following this ceremony, the commander of the troopers, Capitán Tobar, acting for the governor of the province, and "demonstrating the great extent of his Christianity, kissed the feet of the priests and required that all the Indians do likewise, paying obedience to the Supreme Pontiff, visible head of the church. All gave vassalage to the King, our Lord, in whose royal name they were given possession of this place."

The new mission was formally named Santa María de los Dolores de la Punta. The soldiers and Fray Salazar then left to carry official notice of the founding of the mission to the governor, the colegio, and the viceroy. Padre Hidalgo stayed on to carry forward the work at the new mission until Salazar could get back. He set to work with great eagerness, building shelters, preparing fields, teaching the Indians the catechism, and doing the hundreds of other tasks that were needed.

Mexico City was a long seven hundred miles from Lampasos Springs, and Hidalgo had to carry on alone for more than two months while Friar Salazar made the fourteen hundred mile trip on foot or by a plodding burro. As usual, no supply of food and supplies had been furnished to carry the new mission until its own fields and herds could sustain it. So, by the time Salazar got back, Hidalgo was already on a diet of lean, stringy jackrabbits, field mice, and cactus. Nevertheless, he was happy. He had expected the hardships. For him they were mere annoyances, and he had been through worse ones before. He was once again content to be working with the heathen savages of his dreams, and he was a few leagues closer to the land of the Tejas. To this extent, at least, his prayers had been answered.

By the end of its second year, the fields at the new Mission Dolores finally began to yield ample crops of beans and corn and peppers to eat and cotton to weave. Likewise, the mission herd was doing well and increasing. But now that the mission seemed to be a success, Friar Hidalgo began to get restless once more.

He must have reminded himself, "I am forty years old! I have been in New Spain for almost twenty years now. Yet I still haven't really begun the work I was called to do. Before I know it, I'll be an old man. Time is running out!" A new sense of urgency seized him. He must begin casting about for some way to make another move. Not to the land of the Tejas, perhaps. But at least another step in that direction.

In the back of his mind he carried a recollection of a river crossing-place seventy-five miles or so north of Monclova. It had struck him as a fine site for a mission when he first saw this spot on his first journey north into Texas — and it was only fifty miles from the Río Grande! Furthermore, Indians from that area had come to the new Mission Dolores from time to time, to look with envy at the fields of beans and corn growing there. Some even asked the friars how they could get a mission for their area, too, and of course this did not escape the alert Hidalgo.

A plan gradually took form in his mind, and he began a campaign to enlist the aid of Salazar. He finally succeeded in convincing Salazar, so the two friars wrote a joint letter to the governor in Monclova, and another to the colegio, urging that they be given authority to found a mission at the place.

"It is quite suitable for a mission and pueblo," they wrote. "In the area there are many nations of heathen Indians who have desire and enthusiasm for gathering themselves to our Holy Faith and placing themselves in a village and being settled in the society of our Holy Mother Church and to the obedience of His Majesty."

The governor already had permission from the viceroy to found some additional new missions at suitable locations, so the request did not have to go to Mexico City, and it was quickly approved by the governor. Declaring that "the new mission would serve to extend the Faith and be a benefit to the Crown," the governor named an aide, Juan Martín Treviño, to act for him in surveying the site, and if he found it suitable for the mission, to act for the governor in delivering possession of it to the friars.

In due time Hidalgo, Fray Salazar, Treviño with a platoon of cavalrymen, and some Indian guides journeyed to the spot selected. Treviño made an official report of what then happened, which has been preserved and may be found in the National Archives of Mexico. It says, "On June 23 (1699) preparations were made for building a hut in which to celebrate Mass, and for founding the village, by virtue of the commission which I hold for this purpose. Said hut was built, large and capacious.

"On June 24 of said year, day of the glorious precursor San Juan Bautista (St. John the Baptist) the Reverend Fathers Friar Diego de Salazar y San Buenaventura and Friar Francisco Hidalgo rang a bell at the door of the hut. At the sound of the bell more than 150 Indians gathered. There were men, women, and children of the Chaguanes, Pachales, Mescales, and Sarames nations.

"Father Friar Diego, filled with enthusiasm, visited the site, and appropriately, a cross was erected in the earth. The father took off his shoes and worshiped it and sang the hymn. . . . With the prayer of the raising of the cross, he raised it high. In the name of His Majesty he delivered it to me. I kept us in procession until the cross was placed on the altar which was made in the hut for the celebration of the holy sacrifice of the Mass. He finished vesting himself and the Mass was sung, for which the said Father Friar Francisco Hidalgo was minister. After the Mass was finished, he bade them pray the prayers of the Christian doctrine and make the profession of faith, and sing the *Alabado* (chant of praise for the Most Holy Sacrament)."

Following this ceremony, Treviño spoke to the Indians through an interpreter. He told them of "the great care and solicitude which the Catholic Majesty of our Lord and King, Don Carlos II, has for serving God." Treviño went on to say that the monarch had sent missionaries to teach the Indians the Christian doctrine in order that their souls might be saved. "Where the faith and doctrine have been embraced, the people enjoyed great benefits; peace and justice, personal safety, lands and waters for their villages and fields. They were even taught to be polite by the missionaries," Treviño added, "and to wear clothes and shoes. With all these advantages went the knowledge of the Holy Catholic Faith and obedience to His Majesty."

Treviño then cautioned the Indians that they must preserve and fulfill the precepts of the church and abide by the teachings of the friars. They must give obedience to the King and keep his laws. As a result of this speech, Treviño wrote, the Indians "showed great desire and fervor." He was also pleased with the site chosen, saying that it was fertile, had abundant pasture and firewood, and that crops of corn, wheat, and beans could be grown.

When he finished speaking, the officer led the two friars and the Indians outside for the colorful ceremony of delivery of possession of the land. This consisted of walking across the site, having the Indians take water from the stream to sprinkle over the earth, then to pick up dirt and throw it into the air, and to cut branches from the trees, all these being symbolic acts of ownership.

When all this was done, Treviño declared that "adjusting myself in every circumstance to the Royal ordinances and my commission, for the greater reverence of God and His Most

Holy Mother, the Virgin Mary, our Lady and Advocate, I founded on this site this *pueblo* and mission, and placed upon them the names of San Juan Bautista and Valley of Santo Domingo."

As his final official act, Treviño named Padre Hidalgo as missionary in charge of the new mission, and reported that "he remained there with great pleasure and rejoicing."

When the formalities had been completed, Treviño and his soldiers left for Monclova, while Fray Diego returned to his post at Mission Dolores. So Hidalgo was left alone to finish the work of putting the new mission into operation. He could not know it, of course, but his labors were helping to set the scene for the next act in the story.

7/A Sly Trick

Padre Hidalgo worked alone at the newly established Mission San Juan Bautista for a time, building huts, preparing fields, digging ditches for irrigating. It was already the latter part of June — midsummer — and too late to plant crops for harvest that same year. The summer heat and dry weather had set in, and the Indians used the searing heat as an excuse for refusing to work.

After a while two other friars arrived to help Hidalgo, but signs of trouble ahead had already appeared. In addition to the usual lack of a supply of food to carry the mission for a year or two until its own fields and flocks could come into production, the Indians of the region were a growing problem. With no soldiers in the vicinity, the mission had no protection against marauding natives.

To make things worse, at least four different tribes lived in the area around the mission, and even the converts brought their old tribal hatreds with them when they came to live at the mission. Savage fights often broke out between groups of the converts, and the friars had no way to control these outbreaks. Before long, one of the fights left an Indian dead, and after that the hostile tension grew worse.

Finally, one night a friendly Indian woke Fray Hidalgo to warn him of a coming attack. He insisted that the white-skins flee, but the friars were unwilling to desert their mission, and hesitated. It quickly became clear that the danger was very real, however, and instead of defending their new homes, the few converts either ran away or joined in the attack. The friars had to run for their lives, and as they fled into the night, an orange-colored glow arose behind them. The Indians had set fire to the grass huts and chapel.

Mission Dolores was a little closer than Monclova, so the missionaries headed across the arid plain toward it, groping through the dark. When daylight came and they were sure the Indians were not chasing them, they stopped to review the situation. Their decision was to keep on toward Dolores, but to send the older and most senior, Fray Olivares, to report the attack to the governor in Monclova and ask him for soldiers to guard them and help to rebuild the burned mission.

Certainly Padre Hidalgo had no thought of abandoning his mission, as the historian of the colegio makes clear, "or the pagan souls which lived in darkness. The spirit of these operators could not be appeased without looking for new harvests in which they could employ their talents."

Fray Olivares found that a new governor had taken over the post in Monclova, General Francisco Cuervo y Valdés. As a military man, he was better able to visualize the frontier problems than former governors. While Hidalgo waited restlessly at Mission Dolores, several weeks of delay occurred, but when the general did act, it was with vigor. He ordered Major Diego Ramón, a veteran soldier with much frontier experience, to take a troop of cavalry and go back with the friars. He was to protect them and to reestablish the destroyed mission at a location which met with his approval, and also whatever villages or other support he deemed necessary.

The orders to Major Ramón were quite vague, and left almost everything to his judgment. This vagueness was no doubt intentional, for the governor and the major were army officers who knew each other and trusted each other. When Fray Hidalgo saw the instructions, however, he quickly realized that their loose wording might give him an unexpected chance to make another step north — toward his goal of the land of the Tejas.

For ten years he had carried in his memory the ford across the Río Grande, where the entrada into Texas had lost most of its supplies and horses. It would be a good place for a mission and settlement. The land had looked good, and there would be plenty of water. Moreover, he was sure that it would appeal to Major Ramón because of the military value of a settlement to guard the ford across the great river.

We have no means of knowing the details of just how the wily Hidalgo went about persuading Major Ramón and his fellow friars to go along with his scheme. He and the major were friends. They had known each other for many years. The officer already knew of the place, too, for he had been with the expedition that went into Texas to search for the French. Perhaps all of the party thought, or hoped, that the Río Grande Indians would be more peaceable. All we know for sure is that the party passed right by the ashes of the burned mission, and continued on more than fifteen leagues — about fifty miles — to the banks of the Río Grande. There they selected a new site for rebuilding Mission San Juan Bautista.

Government records of the moving or relocation of San Juan Bautista are notably missing, although an account does appear in a history of the colegio written by Friar Isidro Félix de Espinosa. Unlike Treviño, Major Ramón apparently failed to report his actions or the change of location to the viceroy or the governor in an official document. This scarcity of official records lends some support to the theory that the whole thing was a sly trick, perhaps engineered by Hidalgo, to push the chain of missions closer to Texas.

Doubtless Major Ramón and the missionaries knew full well that little was known in Mexico City, or even in Monclova, about the country. No maps of it existed. So the change from one river bank to another, even fifty miles farther north, was not likely to be detected by the Spanish officials.

The new site chosen for the mission is about thirty miles downstream from the present-day cities of Eagle Pass, Texas, and Piedras Negras, Mexico. Today the location is near the small town of Guerrero, Mexico — perhaps actually within its boundaries. In his account, Isidro Felix de Espinosa says: "They arrived at some marshes some two leagues from the Río del Norte (Rio Grande) on January 1, 1700, Day of the Circumcision of the Lord. They named this site the Valley of the Circumcision, and with more than five hundred Indians of the same nations which they had gathered on the Sabinas River, the first mission, San Juan Bautista, was planted, restoring the name which had been used previously."

Major Diego Ramón was pleased, for the site was far enough from the river to be beyond the reach of its floods, yet near enough to command and guard the two nearby fords. The upland between the Sabinas River and the Río Grande was mostly an arid plain, broken here and there by high, rocky hills. On much of it only prickly pear cactus, creosote bush, stunted mesquite, and *lechugilla* grows. In contrast, the soil in the floodplain of the river where he placed the mission was very fertile when irrigated, and water was plentiful.

Like the surrounding country, the climate was hot and dry in the warm season, with frequent sand storms. Both the Spaniards and the Indians often suffered from a weakness which today we would recognize as due to the constant sweating that drained their bodies of salt and water. While winters were mostly mild, sudden "northers" often swept down, bringing numbing cold from the great plains to the north. During these blizzards horses and cattle as well as people suffered a great deal, for neither the animals nor the men were used to the cold. In describing the climate, the historian already mentioned says that it is "very much that of our Spain, of which it is said that there are four months of winter and eight of hell."

Despite its appearance, when water reached it the land quickly sprang into bloom. The air was pure and healthful. Ailments "such as chills and rheumatism" which were common among the Spanish in damp climates, were rare here. Along the streams pecan and walnut trees yielded heavy harvests of nuts, while blackberries and wild grapes were abundant. Major Diego Ramón immediately decided that he would apply for a grant of land in the area. In later years he did this, and started a ranch on his grant.

The friars and soldiers set to work building mud and straw shelters and a hut to serve as a chapel for Mass. In due time, Padre Hidalgo took charge of the mission, and thus began the year 1700. Thus also began a new era in the life of the humble friar, now well past forty years of age. This new era would at times be as stormy and eventful as those which had gone before, but productive nevertheless.

The major concluded that it would be wise to have two missions in this area, to support each other and better guard the important river crossings. Acting under his loosely worded orders, he explored the vicinity and chose a site for a second mission several miles upstream from the first. The story of this new mission is of much interest, for not only did Padre Hidalgo take part in its founding, but also it was destined to be moved to what is now San Antonio, Texas, and there, in time, become the famed Alamo of immortal glory.

It is significant that Major Ramón made a complete report to the viceroy and the governor of this second mission, and this report has been preserved in archives of Mexico, in contrast to the complete absence of any report on Mission San Juan Bautista.

In his report, the major wrote: "In the Valle de la Circuncisión, on the first day of the month of March, 1700, I, Major Diego Ramón . . . placed for execution the founding of a new mission, some two leagues, more or less, from the banks of the same river . . . on a pleasant and fertile site, with abundant land and much facility, on the source of water for irrigation. I brought with me, with the assistance of Padre Predicador Fray Antonio de San Buenaventura y Olivares and of Padre Fray Francisco Hidalgo, the heathen Indians gathered from the land within by means of thc most sufficient diligence of myself as well as by Father Antonio."

After describing how he swore in an interpreter, and other details, Major Ramón goes on: "Thus I told the interpreter that he might give them to understand, first that His Majesty, God keep him, would favor, protect, and succor them with the motive of converting them to the Catholic Faith and to obedience to him, and for their usefulness which will follow the salvation of their souls so that, at the end of their days on earth, they may enjoy the benefits of eternal life."

The friars then took over the ceremony, and proceeded in much the same manner as already described in relating the founding of other missions. They rang a hand bell, then led the recital, by those who knew them, of the four principal prayers with the profession of faith. They then sang hymns of praise, and finally celebrated Mass. Major Ramón concludes his report by saying, "Everyone gave obedience . . . to the Reverend Father Missionary, who would order them in the service of God and King and the increase of their

View of the front (façade) of the ruins of the church of Mission San Bernardo, near Guerrero, Coahuila, Mexico, founded in 1700. The part, with a dome, on the left probably was the baptistery; on the right side there seems to have been a tower. (*Photo by Killis P. Almond Jr., Sept., 1972; courtesy of Maria F. Balderrama.*)

pueblo, by virtue of which I make this edict of foundation."

Even though they understood little of what was said, or the full meaning of the occasion, the savages seemed to be pleased, according to the major. Next he went through the ceremony of delivering the land, announcing that, "for the great honor of God and of His Most Holy Mother I found this site and place this pueblo and mission, and give it the name San Francisco Solano. In the name of His Majesty I give it the civil and criminal jurisdiction which is accorded the other pueblos and missions of this province."

Evidently more thorough than Treviño had been, Major Ramón marked out the site of a village at the new mission, designating the spots where church buildings, cemetery, convent, hospital, the main plaza of the town, and a building for jail should be built. Finally, with the aid of the friars, he selected certain braves from among the Indians to be officials of their community and to enforce the laws.

Fray Hidalgo was formally placed in charge once more of the rebuilt and relocated Mission San Juan Bautista. Friar Antonio was put in charge of the new mission farther upstream, San Francisco Solano. Then, having done his duty, and carried out his vague orders, Major Ramón and his troop of cavalry mounted their horses and rode away, to return to Monclova.

8 / At San Juan Bautista

As always seemed to be the case, the newly moved Mission San Juan Bautista and its sister Mission Solano a few miles upstream, got off to a bad start. San Juan Bautista was laid out on New Years day — in the dead of winter. Mission Solano was established in March. Many months would pass, therefore, before crops of beans and corn could be grown and harvested. Yet there was no stockpile of food and other supplies to carry them over until then.

Padre Hidalgo set to work at once to get a field prepared and seed planted. The spring season proved to be rainy, and even with some help from the Indians, such as it was, this was a struggle. The mission Indians, the converts, had little sympathy with this folly of the whiteskins. They could not see why a crop should be planted when it could not be harvested for many months. They wanted to eat the seed corn, not plant it. And even when a harvest was gathered, they could not understand the reason for storing and saving any of it, either to use for seed or for later eating. "They want to consume what they have the same day they receive it," the friar once wrote. "Nor are they grateful for the blessings they receive."

At last Hidalgo succeeded in getting in a field of corn and beans, and in late spring enjoyed the reward of seeing the corn stalks sprout and begin to reach upward from the virgin soil. But when the plants had reached a height of only about a foot and were still tender, a sudden spring storm struck. The helpless friar had to stand shivering in the door of his hut, watching while the wind and torrents of rain beat the young stalks down.

Even worse than all this was the trouble with the savages, for the situation proved to be no better here than it had been at the first site of San Juan Bautista. Much as he liked the Río Grande country, when his official task was complete, Major Ramón had to leave. General though their language was, his orders could not be stretched enough to give him authority to stay and defend the area. Doubtless he and the two missionaries hoped that the Río Grande Indians would be less hostile than those on the Sabinas, but it did not happen this way.

Conditions quickly reached the point where Padre Hidalgo and Padre Antonio wrote a joint letter to the governor to report the harassing raids by the Indians from both sides of the river. These heathens, they told the governor, were "the instruments of Satan" who worked to "occasion discord," and "to see that the good of those souls is not advanced, the honor of God less visible."

After describing how three or four savages raided the food supply, and then killed ten goats, the letter relates how the culprits were caught by some of the mission Indians — the converts. The raiders then tried to persuade the Christian Indians to kill the missionaries.

This letter makes it evident how much their previous failures weighed heavily on the minds of the friars. They "pray to Your Lordship and ask for God our Lord, and our Father St. Francis, to look after these creatures, that they may not be completely lost, and that we might not be obliged to leave them. It would be a pity for the work to be wasted.

Doorway to the courtyard of an old home in Guerrero, Coahuila, Mexico, the town where the Presidio and Mission of San Juan Bautista were situated in the eighteenth century. (*Photo by Killis P. Almond Jr., Dec., 1972; courtesy of Maria F. Balderrama.*)

The goal is not attained by beginning works but by finishing them."

Urgent as it was, the plea went unanswered. In desperation the two padres finally decided that one of them should make the long trip to Monclova to plead with the governor face to face for help. Since Fray Antonio was much older and not nearly as strong, Hidalgo set out to make the hundred and twenty-five mile walk.

When he reached the provincial capital, it is likely that Fray Hidalgo needed all of his eloquence to persuade the governor. He succeeded, however, and the governor wrote a letter to the viceroy regarding the situation on the frontier. In it he recommended that the missions be given a permanent garrison of at least fifty soldiers, "to serve as guards, custodians, and halter for the barbarous nations which molest the dominions of His Majesty."

Such a garrison would not only protect the missions, the governor pointed out, but would also be of value in "the total correction and defense of this entire province, as well as the adjoining province of Nuevo León, and especially the mining camps at Boca de Leones, Saltillo, Parras, and others." The governor added, doubtless at the prompting of Padre Hidalgo, that Indians from beyond the Río Grande had reported that the French were building settlements on a river in the country of the Tejas. An advanced military post might help in preventing this historic enemy of Spain from edging into Spanish territory.

Turning to other needs of the missions, the governor told the viceroy that each new mission needed a hundred fanegas of corn (a fanega was about 1.6 bushel), to carry it through the period until its own crops could begin to sustain it. Each should be furnished with six large axes for cutting trees and clearing land, six hoes for digging irrigation ditches, three plowshares, one adz, one chisel, and three yokes of gentle oxen for cultivating the fields.

In addition, the governor wrote, the Indian chiefs and officials might be given some clothing which would encourage them to behave decently. He added that additional savages might be attracted to the missions with gifts of tobacco, turnips, strawberries, and the small bells that the Indians liked to wear.

This letter from the governor reached Mexico City in due time, but an aide in the office of the viceroy put it aside for three weeks before reading it, then took another three months to study it before he made up his mind what kind of report to attach to it before giving it to the viceroy. Meanwhile, of course, conditions in the isolated missions got worse and worse.

Returning to San Juan Bautista from Monclova, Hidalgo resumed his duties while he waited and waited for help. Knowing that the missions had no defense, the Indians grew bolder. When the garrison of soldiers which they expected, did not appear, they knew that they could rob, kidnap, or massacre without fear of punishment.

The raids by the "gentiles" caused such terror among the mission Indians that many of them fled to their former wild life. Now and then the converts turned on the attackers and defended themselves and the mission, but this did not happen often, and certainly not often enough to deter the raiders.

Actually, there was little to hold the converts at the missions. Once the novelty wore off, and the awe of the gray-robed friars faded, the natives saw that food was scarce and that they were exposed to the constant threat of attack. Even a bountiful supply of food would not have held them.

Meanwhile, the governor's letter made slow progress through official red tape. Finally the missionaries had a meeting with the bishop, who was making a tour of inspection in Coahuila. The bishop then wrote the viceroy about protection for the missions, and Padre Antonio made the long journey to Mexico City to present the letters in person. The viceroy at this time was an able and forceful man, the Count of Montezuma. When he finally did get the letters and read them, he was impressed by their pleas, and took action at once.

Soldiers were much too scarce in New Spain to furnish a garrison for each mission and village. Still, the Count had a good grasp of military strategy, and hit upon a scheme that made the best use of his sparse forces. He needed to guard larger areas with smaller numbers of troops. This could not be done by a static defense where soldiers wait behind the walls of a fortress for an attack. An active, mobile defense was called for which could move fast and keep the enemy off balance with surprise thrusts.

The plan he devised called for such a mobile force of cavalry, to be stationed at a central point whence it could move quickly in any direction. Thus it could intercept and punish or chase away, any marauding bands of Indians before they could organize an attack in force. Calling this troop a "flying company," the Count ordered that it be sent to the frontier at once, that it be based near Mission San Juan Bautista, and that it be commanded by the veteran Major Diego Ramón, with whom we are already acquainted. Thus was founded the Presidio of San Juan Bautista.

9/Life in a Frontier Mission

A pause at this point to take an overall look at life in a typical frontier mission may aid in a clearer understanding of many of the things that happened in the Spanish outposts in the days of Padre Hidalgo.

As we have seen, one of the first buildings to be erected was always a church or chapel, frequently a mere hut of sticks and mud walls and a thatched roof. This was replaced as soon as possible by a larger building either of logs or adobe bricks, depending on what was available in the vicinity. The final, permanent structure was built of stone and adobe, with massive walls sometimes as thick as four feet. The sturdy beauty of many of the old missions that still stand today is proof of the skill and patience of the Spanish friars.

Other buildings followed the church as soon as possible — more suitable living quarters for the friars and a variety of buildings for use as workshops and storage. As soon as they could, the friars also built a wall to enclose all the buildings and the cemetery. Often a tower rose over each gate in this wall as well as above each corner. Whatever the details in each case, the whole quadrangle was built with an eye to defense against attacks.

Years would pass before a mission reached such a finished state, of course, and in many instances the missionaries lived in the first mud and straw huts for months and even years.

Their task in a new mission was much harder because the friar had to be laborer, architect, foreman, artist and decorator, recruiter of helpers, and teacher of the Indians who knew nothing of the building arts.

The nearest foundries were hundreds or even thousands of miles away, so nails were truly worth their weight in gold. A set of hinges for a door cost more than a horse. Often the timbers for rafters and beams had to be cut in distant forests and then carried by the Indians on their shoulders for many miles across desert wastes. As a natural result, local materials were used as much as possible. Nails were replaced by wooden pegs, and other things were similarly improvised.

When finally complete, a finished chapel contained a richly carved altar, and on it were ornate candle-holders and other vessels of gold and silver for the sacred services. In every corner or niche stood a statue of a saint or a painting of a Biblical scene. Crude homemade benches, a confessional, and other furniture were added as quickly as they could be made.

Outside the chapel, but within the walls of the enclosure, were carpenter and blacksmith shops, a place where the Indian women could weave cloth, and a building for storing the harvests. The food storehouse had to be built strong, for as already mentioned the Indians never seemed to understand completely either that it was sinful to steal, or the reasons why a crop should be stored and saved for a future day.

The granary where the harvest of food crops was stored was kept locked, and the key was kept by the friars. Once a week a ration of food was served out to each family of converts that could be trusted with it. Those who had not been at the mission long enough to learn how to save even a week's quota were given a small daily ration until they could be taught better habits. When a new crop was ready for harvesting, any food that remained in the storeroom from the old crop was sold to the settlers or soldiers. The friar stood by during all bargaining to see that the Indians were not cheated.

As a rule, the Indian women learned to weave on the home-made looms without difficulty. With a little coaching and practice, they soon made cotton and woolen cloth of a fairly good quality. Likewise, after a period of training for the natives, a good grade of pottery often came from the kilns.

An open space near the center of the walled quadrangle served as a place for meetings — and for visiting under the watchful eyes of the friars. Inside the enclosure, the huts of the Indians crowded along the walls of the mission. Beyond the walls, but as near as possible to the mission, were the fields and the pastures for the flocks of sheep, goats and cattle. Corn, beans, Irish potatoes, sweet potatoes, gourds and melons were the most common crops, as well as the ever-present peppers.

An inventory which has survived the passing of centuries and is still in the Mexican archives where it can be read, says that at the time it was taken one of the missions had, "21 yoke of oxen, 24 plows, 61 large hoes, 5 small hoes, 12 iron shovels, 34 hatchets, 8 crowbars, and 12 scythes." In the pastures were "439 head of cattle, 542 sheep and goats, 11 horses, 12 mules and 22 burros." This, of course, was a large and long-established mission.

Some of the huts of the converts, built along the mission walls, were mere lean-to shelters of sticks and mud. Others were sturdier and more elaborate, showing the energy and skill of the family that lived in them. At night everyone came into the walled compound, and the friars closed the

MAP SHOWING AREAS OF HIDALGO'S
EARLY MISSIONARY WORK
RÍO GRANDE (Río Bravo Del Norte)
LA SALLE'S
FT. SAINT LOUIS
LAMPAZOS
MONCLOVA
SAN BERNARDINO
BOCA DE
LEONES
SALTILLO
GULF
OF
MEXICO
ZACATECAS
QUERÉTARO
MEXICO
CITY
VERA CRUZ
PUEBLA
Scale: ½" equals 80 mi.
(or 32 leagues; or 130 km.)

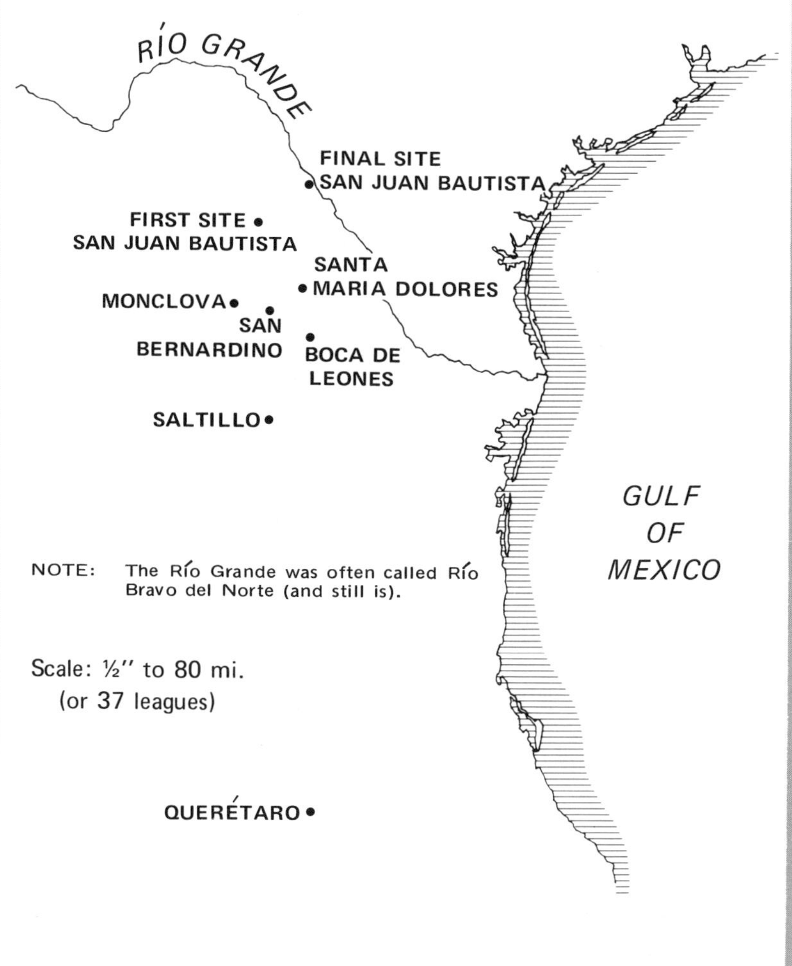
MAP OF MISSIONS FIGURING IN MIDDLE PERIOD
OF LIFE OF FRIAR FRANCISCO HIDALGO
SITE OF
ABANDONED MISSION
SAN FRANCISCO DE LOS
TEJAS
RÍO GRANDE
FINAL SITE
SAN JUAN BAUTISTA
FIRST SITE
SAN JUAN BAUTISTA
SANTA
MARIA DOLORES
MONCLOVA
SAN
BERNARDINO
BOCA DE
LEONES
SALTILLO
GULF
OF
MEXICO
NOTE: The Río Grande was often called Río Bravo del Norte (and still is).
Scale: ½″ to 80 mi.
(or 37 leagues)
QUERÉTARO

gates behind them. While this was done for reasons of safety, it also had the advantage of keeping the Indians from running away.

The daily routine at the mission began with the ringing of bells by the friars to wake everyone and call them to Mass. Even the young except little children had to attend the service. After the Mass, the friars taught the catechism for a half hour. Everyone then went to breakfast, after which the children went to school, while the women began their work at the looms or kilns, and the men went to the fields or shops.

The friars or a few soldiers stationed at the mission directed all work, and tried to teach the Indians European methods of doing things. Everyone worked all day except for a siesta after lunch, and before the evening meal, the friars gave another half hour or so of instruction in the Catholic doctrines. Unless he was sick, an Indian who missed a church service or class was punished. This was sometimes done by whipping them, in a serious case. The culprit was made to kneel before a cross. Then, with everyone else watching, one of the Indian officials gave him four or five lashes with a whip across the bare back and shoulders. Although this was not really a severe treatment, the culprit often ran away afterward.

The patience of Padre Hidalgo and his fellow friars is amazing. They realized that mission life was a radical change from a nomadic life of hunting and fishing. And the devout friars got an immense pleasure from bringing in and teaching "those drawn from among the briars and savage beasts." Even so they had to forgive constantly many failings of the slow, awkward natives while these became skilled and willing to work, a process that often took years.

One of the biggest obstacles to overcome was language.

In one mission, for example, it is recorded that six different languages were used by the various tribes of Indians represented among the converts. To teach the redskins Spanish, or to learn such a variety of native idioms themselves, was a major task for the missionaries. As one historian says, "the total difficulty which is encountered at every turn in such a diversity of idioms," made the friars despair and "raise their eyes to the heavens, asking light to understand." By signs and through "interpreters" who knew a few words of Spanish, they patiently tried to teach the Indians to speak this tongue as quickly as possible.

When new Indians could be persuaded to come in to the mission, the friar took them one at a time, and through one of the converts as an interpreter, began to teach them "all the truths of our holy Catholic Faith." When the friar decided that the new convert was ready for baptism, this was "conferred with all the solemnity provided by the Roman ritual." In the case of young children, the married soldiers or settlers of a nearby pueblo sometimes acted as godparents.

Desertions by the Indians from the missions were frequent. The discipline of the strange life in civilized surroundings, the unaccustomed work, dreams of their former freedom to wander and hunt and fish, news of kinsmen still enjoying the nomadic life, false rumors spread by outside "gentiles," occasional abuse by an overbearing soldier, were some of the reasons for running away.

When an Indian did slip away during the night, he might travel many leagues before daybreak, when he would be missed at morning prayers. The padre would then take a squad of soldiers, if these were available, and begin a search for the runaway. Usually they would find the fugitive and persuade him to come back. Often the chase was long, however, and meant swimming streams, cutting a path through brush, and traveling without rest through the wilderness or across the endless prairies.

The missionaries also tried to give the Indians some training in civic affairs. Each Indian pueblo was permitted to have its own government, including an alcalde or mayor, a council, and a sheriff. With the friar watching to be sure that all was peaceable and fair, the Indians elected these officials from among their own group.

It is necessary to use the word presidio many times in this narrative. In the context of our story, this meant a fort or army base, a settlement where an army force was stationed. The garrison for the usual frontier presidio in New Spain averaged about two hundred and fifty mounted soldiers, with a commander and other officers. In practice, presidios seldom had their full complements, for such isolated posts were not popular with the troopers. The number of soldiers was rarely large enough to guard the herds and take care of the other defense needs. This fact did not escape the notice of the marauding Indians, of course. To make the shortage more critical, some of the soldiers were taken from their military duties and used to help the friars to supervise the Indians at their work in the fields, to go after runaways, and other unsoldierly tasks.

A traveler in our southwestern states or in Mexico, even today, soon realizes that old Spanish towns are similar to each other in a marked degree. They are clearly built to a standard pattern. The human trait of falling into habits explains some common features of towns, but in the case of the Spanish towns there is a more positive reason for the resemblance. The Spanish laws of colonial days laid down detailed rules for laying out pueblos or villas. They decreed that before any building was done, the village must be completely marked out on the ground, as we have seen Major Diego Ramón doing at Mission San Francisco Solano.

The law prescribed that the town must have a square or oblong plaza, and from the four sides of this the streets should lead off at right angles. The parish church, the town hall or cabildo, and other important buildings were to be around the plaza and facing it. These and other rules insured order and geometrical beauty, as well as providing for easy defense, and were followed in all of the towns and settlements with which we are concerned in this story.

What has been said in describing the life in a typical mission should not be taken as applying literally to Fray Francisco Hidalgo in San Juan Bautista or the other early missions where he served. None of those we have mentioned up to now had reached beyond the mud-and-stick-hut stage during his service. The typical mission life that we have pictured should therefore be thought of as something toward which he was striving — a goal he was trying to reach — as he founded those early missions and carried them through their first months and years.

Interior of the Church of Santa Cruz, Querétaro, Mexico. Father Francisco Hidalgo was the superior (Father Guardian) of the missionary college adjoining this church from 1701 to 1703. (*Courtesy of M. A. Habig.*)

10 / The Guardian

By the time the news of the viceroy's decision reached San Juan Bautista, Padre Hidalgo was once more feeling that he had come to the end of his means. A lesser man would have given up long before and abandoned the struggling mission on the Río Grande.

The "flying company" to be based at San Juan Bautista to protect it and the other missions in the area, together with the supplies and tools being supplied at the orders of the viceroy, promised to solve most of the problems. It would be seven months before the troopers, or even food, actually arrived at the needy outpost, however, too late for Hidalgo to welcome them and enjoy the benefits. For in November, when he had been at the mission for eleven months, he received new orders from the colegio.

We can visualize the lonely friar as he greeted the courier who rode up to the mission, carrying the mail from Querétaro. Hidalgo's first thoughts would be of the tired rider and his horse. When they were given water and food, he would retire into his primitive hut to read the letters in privacy. Breaking the seal of wax on the first one, he unfolded its parchment sheet and began to scan it. It was from the colegio, signed by his old friend Fray Antonio Margil. It directed Hidalgo to come to the colegio as soon as he could, as he had been chosen to be his successor as guardian or superior.

Hidalgo was stunned. He could not believe what he read. "Surely there is some mistake here!" he exclaimed aloud. His hand shook as he read the letter once more, slowly this time, pronouncing each word aloud. There was no mistake. Lifting his eyes he fingered the crucifix that dangled at his waist and said, "Lord, I am not worthy of this honor. I am not fit for such a high office. Deliver me from this trial, O Lord! I want only to stay here — to labor among my redskin children."

It was the practice in the Franciscan order to elect a guardian or superior for a term of only three years. But it had never occurred to Hidalgo that he would be chosen for this office. He had been much too busy, his mind too occupied with his work and his dreams, to be conscious of the passing of time. Now, suddenly, he realized with a shock that he was a "senior" friar!

"Of course!" he muttered. "That's why I was chosen! I'm forty-two years old! Twenty-seven years have passed since I entered our holy order. And I've been here in New Spain for eighteen." He thought back over those eighteen eventful years. The burdens and the worries of those years had been many, but his faith, his hopes, his dedication to his work, had made them pass quickly. "I know that I am not fit for this high post. Yet it is true that I am as old now, and as experienced, as many who have held it."

As the first shock from the unexpected news wore off, Hidalgo began to think more calmly. Gradually he began to see it in a different light. So awed by the thought of being guardian — so overwhelmed by the feeling of being unworthy — he had not realized at first that this was really a great blessing. "The guardian has power!" he mused. "When he speaks, people listen! Even the viceroy! This is what I've been waiting and hoping for. This is surely the answer to my prayers. Now, at last, I'll be able to do more than hope and pray. Perhaps I can really do something about missions in the land of the Tejas."

He was now suddenly eager. He must lose no time. "I'll leave at once!" he muttered. "Early tomorrow morning!" He spent a sleepless night staring up into the darkness from his hard bunk. At daybreak he caught one of the small burros from the mission herd and prepared to start the long two hundred fifty league trip. But before he turned the little animal's head south toward Querétaro, Hidalgo turned back for one last look across the Río Grande. How many hundreds — thousands — of times he must have stood thus, looking with longing across the great river toward the north — the far-off land of the Tejas.

With a deep sigh he turned back toward the trail and gently slapped the little burro to start him. Before him stretched an arid, brown, cactus-dotted waste, but his mind was filled with the picture of a vast stretch of rolling red clay hills covered with tall pines. Hidalgo was too practical to spend much time in reverie, and he soon began to make plans. "The Count of Montezuma is the viceroy. How can I appeal to him?"

He rode in silence for a time, trying to remember all that he had ever heard about the able and well-regarded Count. Suddenly he remembered something. "Fray Diego!" he exclaimed. The burro turned his long ears back toward his rider at the sound of his voice. "Diego knows the Count! They are old friends. He can talk to the viceroy better than anyone else I know. He's still at Mission Dolores, and I'll send for him as soon as I take over as guardian."

By the time he made the long journey, then took over the office and had the authority to send for Fray Diego, still another event had taken place. Hidalgo received word that

Church and former Colegio de la Santa Cruz, Querétaro, Mexico. The Colegio established here in 1683 was the headquarters of the group of Texas missionaries to which Father Francisco Hidalgo belonged. Another group came from the Colegio at Guadalupe, near Zacatecas, Mexico. (*Courtesy of M. A. Habig.*)

two Indians who had wandered into the Río Grande missions were telling a story of French activity along the border between Louisiana and New Spain. This was news indeed, and he seized upon it as a "celestial favor."

"Notice of the French has never failed to cause a stir in Mexico City, and even in Madrid," he must have reasoned. "Those two Indians will help Diego to arouse the interest of the Count of Montezuma!" So, when he sent the orders to Fray Diego to come to Querétaro, Hidalgo also told him about the Indians at San Juan Bautista and instructed him to bring them with him.

When Padre Diego and the redskins got to the colegio, Hidalgo questioned them. They told him that a party of thirty white men had come to the land of the Nazones. There they traded muskets to the Indians for horses. The two braves also told of other whiteskins who were building houses on the banks of a river beyond the land of the Nazones. Their story was quite vague in most respects, and especially in the location of the Nazones. The best they could do was to say that this tribe lived "two or three days walk beyond the Tejas, toward the rising sun."

Despite its fuzziness, Hidalgo was impressed by the tale, and felt sure that the viceroy would be too. It tended to confirm the uneasy rumors which reached Mexico from time to time of French violations of Spanish domain. While it was easy for him to guess that the activity of the white men might actually be in Louisiana, in French territory, nothing else had been able to arouse the Spanish officials like the fear of the French. The border between the territories had never been marked, or even explored, so why should he cast a doubt on the story the Indians told?

So, Padre Hidalgo, as guardian, sent Fray Diego and the two savages on to Mexico City. His orders were for Diego to tell the Count about the needs of the outer missions, and also to let him hear the story of the Indians and to try to persuade him to renew the work among the Tejas.

As Hidalgo hoped, the account of the redskins aroused an immediate stir. In fact, the viceroy was so interested that he convened a meeting of his entire council to hear the savages tell their story once more. He then sent urgent letters to the governors of the outer provinces, Nuevo León and Coahuila and Texas, ordering them to investigate. Before the Count could take any further action, however, he learned that the king was sending a successor to New Spain to relieve him as viceroy. So he decided to let the problems rest for the moment, so that the new viceroy could solve them in his own way. Thus the promising plan devised by Padre Hidalgo bore little fruit. It was merely another heartbreaking failure.

The new viceroy was Don Francisco Fernández de la Cueva, the Duke of Alburquerque. The present-day city of Albuquerque, New Mexico, is named for this nobleman, although somewhere along the line one of the letters has been lost from the word. In due time, the duke arrived in New Spain and took up the duties of viceroy.

As soon as Fray Hidalgo learned that the duke had reached the capital, he went to Mexico City to make a formal call in his capacity of guardian. He told the duke about the struggles of the frontier missions, of course, and also tried to interest him in the Tejas project. The viceroy listened, and was sufficiently moved to write to King Philip V about what Hidalgo had reported. The king was much too occupied with troubles closer to home to pay much attention to a far-off wilderness frontier, however, and the viceroy's letter brought no response.

The colegio historian states that "Father Hidalgo promoted

vigorously and untiringly during those years the re-establishment of the missions among the Tejas Indians, which he promised without costs to the Royal Treasury." Just how he expected to do this is a mystery, for the colegio had no such sum of money. It is only one more proof of Hidalgo's boundless faith that God would provide the means if he could but get official permission to go ahead.

One after another his efforts failed, and when at last Hidalgo's tour of duty as guardian ended, he still had no results to show for them. He must have been very dejected that October of the year 1703 as he turned over his office to his successor. The only thing left for him to do was to ask that he be sent back to Mission San Juan Bautista once more. This request was granted, and he left at once to return to the banks of the Río Grande.

Many changes had taken place during the three years that Hidalgo had been gone. Many new problems faced him, but he saw sadly that many of the old problems still remained unsolved, too. At San Juan Bautista there was now a presidio. Facing the mission across a dusty, unpaved parade ground or plaza stood a dozen new, flat-roofed, stone and adobe buildings — barracks for the unmarried troopers, quarters for the married, storehouses for powder and other supplies, a corral for the cavalry horses.

Larger by far than the others was a low, rambling building above which the red and gold banner of Spain hung limp in the still, hot air of the desert. This was the *capitanía* — the office and home of the commandant, Major Diego Ramón. In its shade and near the door, an orderly lounged. He was dressed in high leather boots, white pants, a green coat and a peaked leather cap whose front bore a shiny copper plate engraved with the insignia of his regiment.

The mission itself had changed, too. No longer was it a

mere hut of sticks and mud. Now it was a sturdy church with double walls of stone and adobe, a terraced roof of tile, and a stout wall to enclose church, rectory, shops, and cemetery. Another mission, named for San Bernardo, had been built near the great river, so the area now had a chain of three missions as well as the presidio.

Padre Hidalgo lost no time in getting back to work. As always, he gave all of his time and all of his strength to his task. A record of one typical year relates that in addition to the Masses, confessions, and work in the fields and shops, he baptized three hundred converts, performed a hundred and four marriages, and gave the final rites to one hundred and seventy-two who died.

Hidalgo labored thus for three years following his return to San Juan Bautista. In the latter part of the year 1706, a devastating epidemic of smallpox broke out among the mission Indians in the area. Father Antonio Olivares was elected guardian, so he was no longer there and the full burden of leadership in the crisis fell on Hidalgo, in addition to the responsibility for his own mission.

Within a week after the outbreak, dozens of the natives were dying each day. The friars had their hands full trying to doctor those who were stricken, doing what they could to calm and console their terrified families. Hidalgo rarely stopped to rest even for an hour. Actually, he was helpless to do anything to combat the disease, for there was no known cure for it. The best he could do was to try to make the sick ones comfortable while the disease ran its course and the patient either died or his body threw off the disease.

In the history of the colegio, an account of the epidemic describes it in these words: 'The Creator, knowing the little constancy of these miserable Indians in their good intentions, visited them mercifully . . . with an epidemic of smallpox.

The Christians were favored with the holy sacraments of penance and extreme unction, while the heathens were baptized. More than a hundred died."

The account goes on: "Aided by volunteers from the presidio, (the friars) carried food to the sick, for hardly any of the Indians remained on their feet. Those who did were employed at digging graves and burying the dead. They were allowed to rest at intervals because the malignancy of the fever which infested the air was insufferable. When all the members of a family succumbed to the raging disease, their huts and ranch buildings and all that they owned were put to the torch to prevent the spread of the pestilence."

When at last the epidemic gradually began to subside among the converts at the missions, and it seemed that the crisis was over, Padre Hidalgo learned with dismay that it had spread to the savages living in the "wilderness." To the extent that he could spare the time from the mission Indians, he went out into the country "to redeem all the souls he could with holy baptism." He even succeeded in persuading some of the Indians to come in to the missions.

To the savage mind, the illness was a living creature — a demon that they could run away from. As a result of this belief, they abandoned a village or campsite whenever the sickness broke out there. "It is a ridiculous custom which these barbarians observe in the hope of freeing themselves of the smallpox."

When an Indian was found to be covered with the pox, the other Indians placed the victim under a shade, then surrounded him with a barrier of thorns to keep the disease demon confined. Leaving the victim only a supply of water to drink, they left him alone. "If he is not helped and God as father does not succor him, he most certainly dies."

When they fled from a village where the disease had broken

out, the natives scattered thorns along the path behind them to discourage pursuit by the smallpox demon. Thus they hoped that if the demon tried to follow, he might give up the attempt to catch them, or at least be slowed down.

When the epidemic finally died down in the whole area, the number of converts remaining at the missions was so depleted that Padre Hidalgo persuaded Major Ramón to supply an escort of cavalrymen to gather recruits among the heathens of the region and bring them in to replace those who had died.

While Fray Hidalgo struggled with all his problems and tasks at the isolated outpost on the Río Grande, elsewhere the stage was being set for a new act. Events were taking place on the larger scene which would have a great impact on his life and on the wild frontier between New Spain and French Louisiana.

11 / Treason!

The lower, or southern, part of the vast territory drained by the Mississippi River and called Louisiana by the French, lay between the Spanish provinces of New Spain on the west and Florida on the east. Some years after the ill-fated effort by La Salle to start a settlement at the mouth of the huge river, the French succeeded in establishing a colony on Mobile Bay, near the present city of Mobile. This became the capital of the province, and the base from which exploring and trading reached out into the interior.

To the west, a thousand unexplored miles separated Mobile from the nearest settlement in New Spain. No one knew even where the border lay between the French and Spanish domains. Even so, neither of these traditional enemies could bear the thought of allowing the other to encroach even one inch into its lands.

On the eastern side the situation was very different, for the Spanish settlement at Pensacola was a bare fifty miles from Mobile. This made Pensacola a useful listening post for Spain, and one of the duties of the governor there was to keep a watch on the doings of the French. In that era, the two countries were always either actually at war, had been recently, or expected to be soon. Rivals both in affairs of state and in trade, they were always suspicious of each other.

In 1707 the Spanish governor in Pensacola learned that

the French were about to send a band of twenty-five Canadians and a hundred Indians to explore the country far to the west of the Mississippi and to trade with the Indians there. He hastened to write to the viceroy in Mexico City giving him the news, with all the details he knew, such as a report that the party would carry a large quantity of trade goods with them — two or more boatloads.

As soon as the viceroy received the letter from Pensacola, he hurriedly sent out orders to the governors of the frontier provinces to use every means they could to prevent the French from intruding into Spanish lands. He further ordered them, through the use of friendly Indians or in any way they could, to keep a close watch on river crossings and mountain passes (the latter item showing clearly the Spanish ignorance of the country).

About the same time, Padre Hidalgo and his companions at the Río Grande outposts began to hear rumors from the savages across the river that the Tejas tribes were moving west from their old home grounds along the border of Louisiana. It was easy to interpret this as a flight by the Indians from the French, or even as an effort by the Indians to get closer to the protection of the Spanish against the French. Naturally Hidalgo quickly adopted such an interpretation.

The rumors about the Tejas, coming on top of the report from Pensacola, moved Father Guardian Antonio Olivares to undertake a scout expedition into Texas with young Father Isidro Felix de Espinosa. Accordingly, in the spring of 1709, accompanied by Captain Pedro de Aguirre, they crossed the Río Grande at San Juan Bautista and went into Texas as far as the Colorado River, in the vicinity of present day Austin, Texas. Here they turned back, reporting that the Indians they had questioned assured them that the Tejas had not moved, and that they knew of no French invasions. For Fray Hidalgo this was just another disappointment, and he doggedly went ahead with his work at San Juan Bautista.

Some time after the events just described, Hidalgo's old friend, Friar Antonio Olivares, after completing his term as guardian, made a journey to Spain. His mission was to seek the official approval of the king for another Franciscan colegio in New Spain, begun in 1703 at Zacatecas, and to enlist new recruits for the colegio at Querétaro. While the so-called Franciscan "provinces" in Mexico, six in number, also supplied missionaries for work among the Indians, there was a demand for more on the northern frontier.

In Spain, Fray Olivares took occasion to urge the placing of missions in the unsettled lands north of present Mexico, as he had promised Padre Hidalgo he would do. His efforts had no success, however, and when he returned to New Spain he had to tell Hidalgo that one more scheme had borne no fruit.

Thus the weeks, the months, the years passed. The most that Hidalgo could do was to go out to visit Indian villages whenever he could get away from his duties at the mission. The Río Grande was no boundary at this time, and some of his trips took him across the river into present Texas. They greatly heartened him, for even the "hostiles" let him come among them without harm. While they did not welcome him with enthusiasm, they seemed to sense his sincere interest and grudgingly admired this humble whiteskin in the cowled gray robe.

Not only did the friendly reception by the savages hearten Hidalgo, it also reassured him. Whenever the memory of the tragic scene in the forest and old Totonac's rebuke arose to haunt him, he could at least be sure that the failure of the Tejas mission was not his fault. "They did not hate me!" he must have told himself. "The Spaniards, yes — the white-skins, yes. But not me in person. They were devoted to me. I'm sure of it!"

As best he could, through the Indian grapevine telegraph and from hunters he chanced to meet, he kept in touch with the Tejas. As the months and the years slipped away, however, the prospect of ever going back to them seemed to be less and less real. The mighty Río Grande, which had seemed to be such a long step forward when he and Padre Antonio and Major Ramón founded Mission San Juan Bautista, now seemed to be a barrier that he could not get across.

The longer Hidalgo waited, the farther away his goal seemed to be — the more unreachable. Nothing remained strong and virile except his hopes, his prayers, his determination. Yet no matter what apathy and how many frustrations thwarted him, his firm resolve never wavered. And sometimes mere hopes and prayers and resolve alone, if they are sincere enough and strong enough, will drive a man to action. And so it was with Fray Francisco Hidalgo.

It was a simple thing that he did, or so it seems to us as we look back on it. Nevertheless, it changed the course of the history of North America — perhaps of the world. It may be that the humble but stubborn friar had the foresight of genius. Perhaps he was merely clever. He himself would have said that he had divine guidance.

Was it cunning or a desperate gamble? Was it a carefully planned scheme or an impulsive stab in the dark? Was it the foolish act of an obsessed old man or an act done under divine prompting? Was it mere desperation or far-sighted statesmanship? We cannot be sure. All we know is that after nearly twenty years of frustration, Padre Hidalgo took one final step that succeeded finally in changing everything. But it was treason!

If we take the liberty of imagining the scene, we can see the unhappy friar as he sits forlorn in his tiny cell. It is a chill, wintry night late in January. His homemade stool faces a small shelf in the corner which serves as a desk. The stark, box-like cell is in semi-darkness, lighted only by a candle on the shelf before him that flickers in a weak competition with the glow from the charcoal embers in a brazier on the floor behind the friar. This time of year is a melancholy one for Hidalgo, for it marks the passing of another year since that sad winter when he returned to Mexico from the ill-fated venture among the Tejas.

He sighed deeply. "Seventeen years have passed," he reflected. He pictured himself as he was then, dejected but full of resolve to try again, still young and full of hope. "Seventeen years!" he repeated aloud. "It is a shock to realize that it has been so long! I am fifty-two years old. My life is ebbing away. Soon I'll be an old man! Yet I have done no more than reach the Río Grande!"

Desperation seized him. Leaning forward, he cradled his head in his hands. A low moan of despair broke the silence of the cell. Never had he felt more miserable — more defeated. "If I am ever to go back — if my vision is ever to become a reality — it will have to be soon. But what more can I do? I've tried everything — every device — every scheme! But all to no avail. What remains that I have not already done?"

His mind ran back in a quick review of those years. "The only thing that has ever aroused the viceroy — or anyone else — was the French," he muttered. "A French invasion. If it did so in the past, perhaps it might do so one more time. But there is no French threat, or at least none that I can prove. Perhaps if they were enticed to make one — but how could that be done — by me, a lowly friar in a lonely frontier mission?"

He let his mind seek its own channels for a time. "From all I have heard, the French have all the land they want — too much. They want only furs, wild horses, buffalo hides. And mines. The viceroy told me that the real goal of the French is the gold and silver mines in Mexico. But those are many hundreds of leagues from Louisiana. Much nearer to them is the supply of wild horses and buffalo hides in the wild land to the north. But how could I take advantage of any of that?"

Padre Hidalgo straightened up and shifted his position on the hard stool. The Frenchman La Salle came to his mind. La Salle had landed on the Texas coast and built a fort there. That had certainly caused a furor! "But it doesn't prove that the French were interested in the land. Some said that he was merely lost — shipwrecked. We often hear rumors from the Indians that the French are coming into Texas from Louisiana. But none of our entradas has found any actual trace of them."

His cowl fell back from his head, but he did not notice, and continued to muse. "If only the French would make some move — one that would prod my people. A real move, not just a vague rumor. Something that seemed to be an actual threat. That would wake up the viceroy! And the King! But how could I bring any such thing about? I've already tried everything I could think of."

The chill in the cell made him shiver, and he reached back to pull his cowl up over his head once more. Then his thoughts went back to his problem. "If something called their attention to that country of the Tejas — something that made them realize how unsettled and unguarded it is. Of course, they are busy with their own troubles in Europe, I'm sure. Just as the Spanish are. But the French are clever.

I'm sure they would get ideas if they knew the region was wide open to them. Perhaps if I wrote them a letter! A vaguely worded letter that said little but hinted much more! A letter asking for help in starting missions among the Tejas!"

Hidalgo felt a new warmth come to his face. But then another thought struck him. "But that would be treason! If they really did move into Texas — if a threat grew into an actual invasion — I'd be a party to it! I'd be a traitor! In fact, merely writing to the French would be treason — whatever the letter said, and whatever happened."

This came as a shock, and he had to consider it for a long time. Finally, he sighed once more and mumbled, "But I must do something! What else can I do? This is my last hope!" He sighed again. "All I want is to arouse my people. But only the French can do that. And even if they did intrude a little into Spanish territory, what harm would be done? No one really knows just where the border is. Or cares, to tell the truth. New Spain is already too big for us to settle it, or even to explore it. No, this is my last chance, I know. I must do it. I must!"

His mind made up at last, Hidalgo leaned over to pull the candle closer, reached up to a tiny shelf above him for the ink pot, a quill pen, and a sheet of parchment. Unrolling the parchment, he spread it out on the makeshift desk. "God forgive me for what I'm doing, if it is wrong!" he muttered, and picked up the pen.

His hands were so stiff from the cold that he had trouble in holding the quill. He put it down on the desk, clasped his hands and raising them to his lips, blew on them. The warmth of his breath felt good, but it was not enough. He got up, stepped around the stool and over to the center of the little room. There he squatted down beside the brazier to hold his hands over the glowing charcoal embers — the only heat in the austere cell.

After holding them over the hot coals for a minute, he flexed his fingers, rubbed his hands together briskly, and arose to go back to his writing. Moistening the point of the quill in his mouth, he dipped it into the ink pot. Then bending over the parchment, he began the letter.

Dating the letter January 27, 1711, he addressed it to the governor of the French settlement at Mobile. Then with carefully chosen words, he wrote of his deep concern for the spiritual life and bodily welfare of the Tejas, as well as their neighboring tribes. As he wrote, the words flowed from his pen more easily. He told the governor of his grief that those pagan savages were abandoned in the vast forests of east Texas without anyone to minister to them. He earnestly asked the governor to send him news of his redskin children and how they fared.

He went on to express his own great desire to return to those tribes. Finally, mentioning that the country was near to the French province of Louisiana, he asked for any help possible from the governor in founding another mission among the Indians of the region.

When at last he finished, Hidalgo held the sheet up closer to the candle and read what he had written. Then he went over it, correcting mistakes, and finally rewrote it on a fresh sheet of parchment. Now that it was finished, the thought came to him that it faced heavy odds in the wild country and long journey. He decided to make two more copies so that he could send three identical letters by different couriers and different routes. That would improve the chances that at least one of them might get to its destination.

Even after taking this precaution, he knew better than to let his hopes balloon on the strength of the letter, A thousand miles of wilderness lay between San Juan Bautista and Mobile; and he was not sure that his letter would get a favorable reception by the French. Nevertheless, it made Hidalgo feel good simply to have done something. He had been able to do nothing but hope and pray for so long that he felt relieved to be taking some real action, even though it did not seem to have much promise of success.

So trying to be patient and with caution not to be carried away by hope, he waited. Daily he reminded himself that it would be months before the letter could reach Mobile, if it ever got there at all. And months did pass, many of them. They dragged on into a year — a year and a half — two years. But no reply came. Each day of that endless wait he wondered if the letter had reached Mobile. Each day and each night he prayed that it might be delivered and that its plea might be read by a sympathetic governor there.

Even a hope as steadfast as his dimmed as time dragged on. Another scheme seemed to have failed. His risky letter had gained him nothing. His only comfort was that he had not been arrested for treason, for as time passed, he saw more and more clearly how foolish his impulsive scheme had been. Such treason as boldly writing to a French governor would be dealt with most severely if one of the copies of the letter should fall into the hands of the viceroy — or any Spanish officer. Belatedly he realized that it was better that the letter did get lost than to be intercepted.

At length, two years after Hidalgo sent the letter, his superiors in the colegio decided that he had served long enough in the isolated outpost at San Juan Bautista. He had been there now for fourteen years, broken only by his three year tour as guardian. So they recalled him to Querétaro for a turn in a less arduous post.

The change in duty did not please Hidalgo, however, for

he did not want to leave his work among the Indians. Nevertheless, he obediently bade farewell to Major Ramón, his troopers, their families and the Indian converts who gathered about him to wish him Godspeed. Then he set out over the familiar trail over desert and mountain, for Querétaro.

Arriving at the colegio in due time, Hidalgo settled down in his new post. Here he spent another long year and a half, doing the routine tasks that were assigned to him, before the curtain rose on the next scene in his story.

12 / *The French React*

In the spring of 1713, two and a half years after Fray Hidalgo wrote his letter, a new French governor arrived in Mobile. Called Cadillac in English-language histories, his full name was Antoine de la Mothe, Sieur de Cadillac. An energetic man who had gained much experience around the Great Lakes and on the frontier of Canada, his task was to put the Louisiana colony on a paying basis for the hard-pressed king of France. But he quickly learned that this would not be easy.

The great grassy plains where countless buffalo grazed and herds of wild horses ranged, lay far to the west of Louisiana, and in a region that belonged to Spain. Likewise the fabled gold and silver mines, if they existed at all, were in the mountains of New Spain, hundred of leagues from Louisiana.

It was clear to Cadillac, therefore, that the coveted buffalo hides, the wild horses, the gold and the silver that he needed to make his province pay off had to come through trading, either with the Indians living in Spanish territory, or with the Spanish themselves. He well knew of the stubborn refusal of the Spaniards to trade with foreigners, and his problem was somehow to ignore, or push back the border, or evade the Spanish officials. Indeed, a trickle of illegal trade had gone on across that border for years, but Cadillac had to find some way to enlarge that trickle to a flood if his colony was to be a profitable investment.

The first thing that the new governor decided to try was trade by the sea route between Mobile and Veracruz. Even though beset by pirates and hurricanes, this was the easiest way. So Cadillac fitted out a ship, loaded it with French goods, and sent it across the Gulf of Mexico to trade for livestock and other products. The gesture met with an immediate and stern rebuff. The Spaniards turned the ship back from their port with a sharp warning not to return. The ports of New Spain, they said curtly, were closed to all commerce that was not borne in ships flying the flag of Spain.

So, trade across the border was his only hope after all, and Cadillac cast about for ways to get it. He was more at ease with the Indians, anyhow. He had much experience with them, and like most Frenchmen, was more tolerant and easy-going with them than were the Spanish. The French never tried to move the savages into mission pueblos and teach them European customs. Cadillac was content to leave them as they were, therefore, bartering with them for furs and hides, but otherwise letting them lead their own lives.

This was the situation, then, when at last one of the copies of the wily letter written by Fray Francisco Hidalgo finally came into the hands of the French governor. Cadillac still smarted from the rebuff by the officials in Veracruz; and although the letter was a puzzle to him, he seized upon it as pointing to a way to success by an alternate route.

The governor immediately sent for the most able and experienced man in the colony, an explorer and trader named Louis Juchereau, Sieur de St. Denis. St. Denis, as he is known in histories in the United States, was a French creole — that is, he was born in the new world, of French parents who had migrated to America. A tall, handsome, dynamic man, he spoke a number of Indian dialects and even some Spanish. He had a genius for dealing with the savages, but also got along well with everyone else. In addition, he was a superb woodsman and an expert swordsman.

Once the letter was translated into French, the two men sat down in the log cabin which served as the governor's office, and tried to solve the puzzle of this strange message from an unknown friar. What did it mean? The language was fairly clear, but it was unbelievable. The writer seemed to be sincere, but why didn't he go to his own people for help with the missions? Or if he had done so, why had the Spanish refused to help him? Could this be a trick? The bait in a trap of some kind? All Frenchmen thought that a Spaniard could not be trusted.

As the two men pondered the enigma, other questions arose. Where did those Tejas Indians live? Where is this San Juan Bautista that the friar wrote from? Do the Spanish guard the frontier? If so, how did the letter get through? There was no answer to these questions. Yet the plea from the unknown friar was too tempting — the mystery was too inviting — to let the whole thing drop without trying to learn the answers. The few facts that were known certainly promised that solving the puzzle might be profitable.

For example, missions among the Tejas, wherever the Tejas might be, could perhaps serve as convenient trading points. Haphazard barter with scattered and wandering Indians was not easy or fast. Well-located missions that would evolve into trading posts would make it easier. It was obvious that an outlet for hides and other things would be more logical through Louisiana than over the much longer route to Mexico City and Veracruz, so why not exploit it?

The severe anti-trade laws of the Spaniards might be an obstacle, of course. But even if the border was guarded, it would be harder for this to be effective than in a port like Veracruz. Furthermore, St. Denis and Cadillac agreed, this Fray Hidalgo might know how to evade the strict laws. The French needed very much to explore that country to the west, and to find out if trade with it was possible.

The two men agreed that the best course open to them was for St. Denis to take a party into Texas to explore the country and learn all he could about the Indians, as well as to find this Friar Francisco Hidalgo and talk to him. Only in this way could answers be found to all the questions raised by the strange letter.

St. Denis got together a large pile of trade goods — cloth, beads, knives, mirrors and other articles popular with the Indians. Loading all this into a small fleet of canoes, with a dozen Frenchmen and some Indian guides, he worked his way along the coast to the mouth of the Mississippi, then up that great river to the point where what is now called the Red River empties into it. Here he turned west and followed the Red River as far as he could. Where it turns north, he found the village of a tribe of Indians called the Natchitoches, after whom the present-day town located there is named.

Since he was already as far north as he wanted to go, St. Denis stopped at this bend and unloaded the canoes. There was far too much of the trade goods for the party to carry overland, so they built two log cabins to house the surplus goods and supplies. Then, leaving a squad of men to guard the stored goods, St. Denis took some Indian guides and most of the Frenchmen and struck out through the great pine forests toward the setting sun.

Following old Indian trials, the party traveled a route which later became the historic Old Spanish Road, or Old San Antonio Road. This heavily forested country was very different from the coastal region, but St. Denis pushed on without stopping to explore. After twenty days of travel he reached the Neches River, in the vicinity of the first Spanish mission built by young Friar Hidalgo and Padre Massanet. Burned and abandoned more than twenty years before, there was little trace of it now. St. Denis did find a few horses, cattle, and sheep ranging through the forest, descendants of stock that the Spanish had left behind when they went back to Mexico.

The colorful Indians in the area were very different from the natives of the Mississippi valley, St. Denis reported in a letter to his governor. Like the tribes of the great plains, many "are mounted on horseback, with quivers fastened behind, filled with arrows. They carry a bow and a small shield made of buffalo hide, which is held in the left hand and is intended to protect them from the arrows of their enemies. They have no other curb or bridle for their horses than a piece of hair rope; their stirrups are made of the same material, which are fastened to deerskin three or four inches in thickness, thus forming their saddle."

St. Denis further told Governor Cadillac that "their lands are all cultivated and there are no fruits in the world richer . . . nor more wonderful grapes of various kinds and colors in such quantities. The bunches are as large as twenty-eight and thirty pound shot. There are also such extensive fields of flax that all the fleets of Europe could be supplied with cordage."

St. Denis did not find Padre Hidalgo, of course. The friar was now a thousand miles away in the colegio in Querétaro, and not even aware that his letter of three years before had finally reached Mobile and been delivered to the governor there. Some of the Indians in the vicinity told St. Denis that they remembered the devout, gray-robed friar however, and despite their hatred of Spaniards in general they had liked and admired Hidalgo.

The canny Frenchman found the Tejas so eager to trade with him that he stayed among them until he used up his entire supply of trade goods. The pile of buffalo hides and furs he got grew so high, and the herd of wild horses so large, that nearly all the men in the party were needed to get them back to the base at the Natchitoches village. Only three remained with St. Denis.

Since he had not yet found the letter-writing Hidalgo, St. Denis decided to push on with his three remaining men. The Indians told him of the Spanish settlement on the Río Grande, and thought that Hidalgo might be there. So St. Denis headed for that goal. As guides and escorts, he hired the old enemy of the Spaniards, Chief Bernardino, and twenty-five of his braves.

Following the trail blazed by the Spaniards, the party reached the Colorado River. Here the country became arid and more open, and here an Apache war party of "two hundred hostile Indians" suddenly swooped down out of the hills to attack the travelers "with the furiousness of demons." Under the leadership of St. Denis, the party managed to drive off the Apaches. Then, after scouts reported the trail ahead was now safe, Bernardino and his braves turned back, leaving the four Frenchmen to trudge on southwestward alone.

Another ten days of travel brought them within sight of the pale green line that marked the course of the winding Río Grande through the brown, cactus-studded plain. Soon St. Denis made out the bell towers of the Missions San Juan Bautista and San Bernardo. Another league of walking brought into view the low stone and adobe houses of the presidio. He had finally reached the outpost of New Spain.

Warned of the approaching strangers by his scouts, Major Ramón sent out a patrol to bring them in. Once they were in his office and identified as Frenchman, he demanded that they explain their being on Spanish soil without permission. St. Denis insisted that his visit was peaceful, and that he wanted only to arrange for trade across the frontier. He also mentioned that he was looking for Fray Hidalgo, who had written a letter to the French governor.

At first, Major Ramón did not believe the story. The whole account sounded like a fairy tale — the fantastic journey from Mobile, the purposes of it, the incredible letter from Fray Hidalgo. Yet the voice of the tall Frenchman had the ring of sincerity. His eyes did not waver under the scrutiny of the major. And the commander knew full well how completely Hidalgo was obsessed by the urge to go back to the Tejas. He well remembered some of the schemes that Hidalgo had promoted in the past — such as moving the Mission San Juan Bautista fifty miles north of where it was supposed to be.

Major Ramón realized from the start what this visit and this Frenchman meant, and what a sensation it would cause in Mexico City. And of course the whole incident must be reported to the viceroy at once. It was equally clear that Hidalgo's letter was flagrant treason, and his first impulse was to avoid any mention of this rash act of his old friend. It did not take him long to see that it would be discovered anyhow, however. To attempt to hide it would only make it appear worse when it did come to light.

While the prisoners were being given water and food, the major grabbed up his quill pen and inkpot to scribble a hasty report to the viceroy of the whole affair. He followed this with a report to the governor of Coahuila, and at last wrote a note to Padre Hidalgo telling him about the arrival of St. Denis and of the story he told. These three letters he dispatched at once by a special courier.

This urgent duty out of the way, the major had time to question St. Denis at greater length. Secretly, he was glad to have the charming and refined Frenchman at San Juan Bautista. Life at the lonely outpost was dull and tiring for the most part, and the major was hungry for someone to talk to. Likewise, for the women of his household — his wife and a seventeen-year-old granddaughter — indeed for all the Spaniards at the presidio, the arrival of the strangers was a welcome break in the dreary tedium of their lives.

Since St. Denis was obviously a gentleman, the commander accepted his word of honor that he would not try to escape, and made him a prisoner-at-large. The cultured Frenchman was quickly accepted into the social life of the tiny outpost, too, and in fact his presence touched off a revival of social activity. Nor did it take long for romance to develop between the handsome St. Denis and the dark-eyed Manuela, the granddaughter of the major.

It was not until mid-August of 1714, three weeks after the arrival of St. Denis at the presidio, that Padre Hidalgo received the news from Major Ramón. Three and a half years had passed since he wrote his letter to the French governor, and he had long since given up hope that it had reached its destination. Now, he hurriedly got permission from his superiors to go to San Juan Bautista, and with his mind a turmoil of mixed hope and dread, he set out at once. He must talk to this St. Denis without delay.

13 / Hidalgo and St. Denis

Coming back to San Juan Bautista was always like coming home to Padre Hidalgo. It lifted his spirits. The founding of the mission fourteen years before had been one of the highlights of his life. He had seen it grow from a straw-thatched hut to the present weathered stone chapel with its walled compound of living quarters, shops and granaries.

Across the dusty plaza, where before there had been only a brush and cactus covered waste, now stood the rambling barracks, quarters and other buildings, their sun-baked, drab brown brightened by strings of red peppers hanging from the exposed ends of the rafters to dry. The gay dresses of the Indian women, the bright green and white uniforms of the troopers, the prancing cavalry horses, livened the scene and stirred a fatherly pride in Hidalgo's heart.

When he arrived this time, however, Hidalgo paid little attention to all this. This time his mind was filled with eagerness to find out what message St. Denis brought, and with anxiety about what his own fate would be when the viceroy learned of his rash letter to the French. He and St. Denis liked each other from the start, despite their different natures — the gentle, humble friar, and the tall, dashing soldier of fortune. No doubt each sensed in the other the one trait — an unyielding resolve — that made them kindred characters.

St. Denis related his adventures to Hidalgo, and told him all he knew about his beloved Tejas Indians. He promised the friar any aid within his power in getting missions established in east Texas once more. For his part, Hidalgo pledged to give the likeable Frenchman all the help possible in defending himself against the charges of breaking the laws of Spain.

Although a firm alliance quickly arose between the robed friar and the buckskin-clad adventurer, little could actually be done by either until the viceroy acted. No one doubted that there was great dismay in Mexico City, but that did not mean quick action could be expected.

Meanwhile Hidalgo busied himself in getting as much support as he could for the cause of the Frenchman. It was easy for him to win over the missionaries on the frontier who were exposed to the charm of the stranger. He even succeeded in enlisting the support of the friars at the colegio in Querétaro, convincing them that the prisoner had promised his help in saving heathen souls and that he was a friend who was interested in them and their work. Not so easy to persuade were the higher and more influential clergy, such as the bishop and the archbishop. Even so, Hidalgo was able to bring a considerable amount of influence to bear on the viceroy in one way or another.

St. Denis arrived at San Juan Bautista in midsummer — July 19, 1714. Yet it was not until eight months later, late in March of 1715, that orders came from the Duke of Linares, who was now the viceroy of New Spain. The orders came in the form of a platoon of troopers sent from Mexico City to bring the prisoner in chains to the capital. There the duke would give his personal attention to the case. The size of the guard — twenty-five soldiers — was proof of the importance of the prisoner in the mind of the viceroy.

Also going to the capital with St. Denis was a young officer from the garrison at San Juan Bautista — Domingo Ramón, a son of the commander. The youthful Domingo held the rank of *alférez,* about the same as a modern day second lieutenant or subaltern. His function was to answer any questions that the viceroy might ask about the details of how the party of Frenchmen came to the outpost. Sending young Domingo was a favorable step, for he had grown to manhood under the ministry of Padre Hidalgo. Furthermore, like the entire Ramón family, he was solidly behind St. Denis, now engaged to marry Manuela as soon as he could be released and able to come back to the outpost from Mexico City, as a free man.

The waiting was over for St. Denis, but still no word came from the capital as to the fate of Fray Hidalgo. The nights of tossing on the hard bunk in his cell did not suddenly and mercifully end with news of a decision about his punishment. Instead, he was still left to suffer the tortures of uncertainty as to his own destiny, as well as that of St. Denis. As one writer expresses it, "the Venerable Padre was not pardoned of many mortifications of his spirit."

St. Denis did not fare as well in Mexico City as he had at San Juan Bautista. Upon arrival there he was thrown into a dark and filthy dungeon in the central military prison, still wearing his chains. His bed was a pile of straw on the floor in a corner, his cell mates were huge rats.

At intervals, first of days, later of weeks, a guard marched him to the palace, where some member of the viceroy's staff would question him. In these endless hearings, as well as in a written statement, he told the story over and over again of his journey into Texas, the Indians he had seen and the country he had traveled through. In his disarming way, St. Denis stressed that his innocent purpose was to trade with the Indians and settlements, never thinking that the Spaniards would not be pleased to have goods brought to such isolated outposts.

To promote his plan to use missions as trading posts, as well as his promises to Fray Hidalgo, St. Denis told of the affection that the Indians had for the Spanish padres, and their desire for the whiteskin missionaries to return. Describing in detail the fertile country, he shrewdly emphasized his own knowledge of the land and of the Indians, his ability to speak to the natives in their own tongue, and his own willingness to help the Spanish if they decided to place new missions in Texas. And he never failed to play subtly on the Spanish fear that the French might move into the wide open border region.

After many weary months, the slow-moving inquiry finally reached a climax when the viceroy decided to hear St. Denis in person, and even convened his entire council to listen. The glib St. Denis once more told his story to this distinguished group, then went back to his dungeon to wait some more.

As the months dragged on, there was nothing for Padre Hidalgo to do but wait, as he had already brought all the pressure he could on the viceroy on behalf of St. Denis. He kept abreast of events in the capital through letters from St. Denis, smuggled out of the prison, and from Domingo Ramón. As he went about his duties, he tried to conceal his own anxiety. The expected blow did not fall on his head, but waiting in dread for it was more than a severe punishment for his crime.

What really happened was that the viceroy had decided to ignore the disloyalty of the humble friar who had labored faithfully in New Spain for so many years. But he never did notify Hidalgo of his decision, and Hidalgo knew of it only by guessing as passing time and events made it evident.

At last, in August of 1715, four and a half years after he wrote his fateful letter, news reached Fray Hidalgo of the ruling of the viceroy on St. Denis. The outcome was worth all the waiting — it was all that Hidalgo had prayed for, and more. In a formal decree, the duke approved a new mission among the pagans on the frontier with Louisiana. The edict declared: "By this means, similar (foreign) incursions will be prevented, and what is more important, these Indians will obtain instruction in our holy Catholic Faith and the spiritual welfare of their souls, to which the zeal of His Most Christian and Catholic Majesty is inclined."

The viceroy promoted the youthful Domingo Ramón to the rank of captain and put him in charge of the expedition to found the new mission. St. Denis was freed and appointed to be a guide and adviser for Domingo Ramón. Finally, "Fray Francisco Hidalgo, as the one who most desired the conversion of the Tejas," was to go along with the entrada to the new mission.

The day for which Hidalgo had fasted and prayed and schemed had finally come — after twenty years! But there was even more good news. A few days after the first decree, the viceroy issued a second one, ordering that there be not merely one mission on the Louisiana frontier, but five. And a presidio in a central point in their midst to give support and protection to all of them. To populate the presidio, the soldiers of the garrison were to take their families with them, and also a band of settlers were to be recruited in Mexico to move to it with their families and possessions.

Through these measures, the edict said, the viceroy hoped that a stable and permanent settlement would be formed in east Texas. And in a further effort to give the distant missions the support they needed, the duke ordered that one of the Río Grande missions be moved to San Pedro Springs (San Antonio, Texas), to serve as a half-way point on the road to guard the line of communication.

14 / The Return

Haste was not a Spanish virtue, and there were hundreds of problems for St. Denis and young Domingo in getting the soldiers and animals and supplies and settlers together and ready. Months would still pass before the calloused feet of Fray Hidalgo would tread the soil of Texas once more. But he could force himself to be patient. He had been forced to practice that long enough to be adept at it.

It was February of the next year, six months after the viceroy's decision, before the expedition was finally ready to leave Saltillo, the assembly point chosen for it by the youthful commander. The route ran north through Monclova and on to San Juan Bautista, then across the Río Grande and northeast through Texas. As the long column crept across the barren land, it suffered delay after delay. Now they had to wait for more horses, now to hunt for lost mules that had strayed away; today wait while scouts searched ahead for water holes large enough for the herd of oxen, goats, and sheep — tomorrow wait "for a woman in labor to give birth to a baby."

Two months passed before the marchers camped at San Juan Bautista. Major Diego Ramón came out at the head of his troop of cavalry to receive the expedition with military ceremony and honors. With him came the missionaries now stationed at the three missions in the area or waiting to join the expedition, including Padre Hidalgo. St. Denis, too, was in the welcoming party, for he had hurried back from Mexico City so he could marry Manuela Sanchez and spend a brief honeymoon with her while waiting for the slow moving main body of the entrada group to catch up with him.

On April 10, the crossing of the Río Grande began. Luckily the river was not in flood, and only the sheep and goats had any trouble in fording it. By April 27th, all the people, animals and supplies were across, and the march into the "wilderness" could begin. As the column moved out that spring morning of 1716, it passed in review before its youthful commander. The devout Capitán Domingo Ramón ordered that the missionaries lead the march as a sign that the primary purpose of the entrada was religious. And among them marched Padre Francisco Hidalgo, his face glowing with happy pride, his bearing dignified, his step as firm as it had been that day twenty-five years earlier when he first set foot on Texas soil. His hair had turned gray as he waited, but at last his day of triumph had come.

Next in line came the rest of the eleven missionaries — four priests from the colegio in Querétaro, three from the new colegio in Zacatecas, an oblate and two lay brothers, all plodding along in their somber gray robes. Following these came the officers and St. Denis, mounted on spirited calvary horses. Two years had passed since the tall Frenchman first crossed this great river and walked into San Juan Bautista in his search for Fray Hidalgo.

After their officers came the escort of twenty-five troopers, on prancing horses and with their lances flashing in the bright morning sun. Next were eighty other people — two retired soldiers with their families, seven other families, two mule drivers and ten helpers, three Indian goat herders, two Indian guides — a varied and colorful crowd.

The supply train consisted of eight two-wheel carts, pulled by oxen and creaking under their heavy loads, and a line of pack mules and burros. Last of all came the herded animals — four hundred and ninety burros, mules, and horses, sixty-four oxen, a thousand goats and sheep. As all these animals plodded along in the cloud of dust raised by their six thousand hoofs, the drumming of their steps, the lowing of the oxen, the bleating of the sheep, the groaning and squeaking of the carts, and the shouts of the herders blended into a tumult that could be heard for miles around.

Both Capitán Domingo Ramón and a scholarly friar named Father Isidro Espinosa kept diaries during the march into Texas, and these are still available to us in the Mexican archives. It was spring, and even the brown plain showed it. "We passed a few low hills without trees" and "several marshes with mesquite and Indian fig trees, whose fruit was not ripe." The creeping column was able to cover only a few miles each day, but after about a week they were in the hills and "a beautiful country, a land covered with a variety of flowers with admirable fragrance."

The season was dry, and there was a "depressing heat," even though summer was two months away. The streams and rivers were so low that they were easy to cross. This was a great blessing, but it was sometimes difficult to find water for so many animals. The river bottoms were covered with "an abundance of ash trees, walnut, mulberry, and others of various kinds." Yet "we were hailed by mosquitoes playing their trumpets who entertained us both day and night."

May 3 fell on Sunday, and was the day of the feast of the Finding of the Holy Cross. So Capitán Domingo Ramón ordered a halt for the day. Seven Masses were said, and everyone received Communion. Padre Hidalgo and his fellow friars fashioned a large cross from the limbs of trees, and after blessing it, they carried it in a solemn procession three times around the camp, with all the people of the expedition following behind them.

Luck ran out for the travelers on May 13th, however, when they reached the Medina River. At the point where the trail crossed it, this stream had cut into a high limestone hill, so that the opposite bank had a slick and steep slope. The herders drove some of the horses into the stream and the animals began to swim across. When the leading horses got to the far bank, however, they could not climb up the slippery ledge, and fell back into the river. Before anyone could divert them, the whole herd of swimming horses was milling about in mid-stream. In the ensuing panic, eighty-three of them drowned before the herd could be turned back.

This was a serious loss for the party — almost a fourth of the horses — and "a grievous discouragement among the weaker hearts." The friars concluded that "perhaps the devil had done this to hinder the conflict about to be made against him. To crush him, a High Mass was sung the following day."

In July the slow-moving expedition reached and crossed the Trinity River. Now, at last, they were entering the land of the Tejas, although still a long way from the Louisiana border — some forty leagues. The impatient Hidalgo suggested that the friars, with St. Denis and a few others, go ahead as fast as they could, rather than wait for the crawling supply train and plodding herds of animals. In this way, he told the young capitán, they could sooner select the sites for the missions and begin clearing the forest away for the buildings.

Domingo agreed to the plan, and in fact decided to go with the advance party himself. As they neared their destination, St. Denis hurried on ahead to arrange for some of the Nacogdoches tribe chiefs to get together for a welcome ceremony for the Spanish. This the Indians agreed to do, and they were waiting when the advance party arrived.

The Indians met the capitán and the friars on the trail, then led them into a village where everyone sat down on the ground in a circle around a council fire. The chief of the host village lit a peace pipe with an ember from the fire, then passed the long pipe to Domingo, seated on his right. Taking a puff, Domingo handed the pipe back to the chief, who then handed it to St. Denis, on his left. After St. Denis took a puff, the chief started the pipe around the circle from hand to hand.

When the pipe got back to him, the chief handed it to a young brave who stood behind him waiting to return it to its place in the hut of the chief. St. Denis now nodded to Domingo, and the young leader reached behind him, picked up a leather pouch and got to his feet. Opening the pouch he drew out a necklace of glittering blue stone beads, and with a flourish handed it to the host chief. Then he stepped from one to the other of the remaining chiefs, giving each of them in turn a similar necklace.

This ceremony finished, Domingo went back to his place in the circle, faced the council fire, and with St. Denis translating, spoke. "These gifts I bring as the servant of our great King Felipe V," he began. "By the hands of the Duke of Linares, who is now his viceroy, the king of Spain sends these gifts to our redskin brothers as a token of his love for them.

"Being further concerned for the welfare of your souls, he has also sent these gray-robed medicine men. They make strong medicine with their chants and their candles. They will minister to you and tell you of our God. They will bring you the blessings of the gospel of the Lord.

"Furthermore, in order to insure that no enemy disturbs you, our great king has sent me and these soldiers to guard this land and to administer his laws among you."

When Domingo finished, he once more sat down in his place in the circle. The host chief, followed by each of the other chiefs, then made speeches of welcome. When the ceremony was finally over, all those present seemed to be satisfied with the way things had gone. For his part, Fray Hidalgo was greatly pleased, and felt that a good beginning had been made.

15 / History Repeats

The locations picked for the first five missions and the presidio strung out in a rambling line from near the site of the mission abandoned in 1693 to the present day city of San Augustine, Texas. The distance ranged from about a hundred miles to about fifty miles west of the French settlement at Natchitoches. In order to fully occupy the area between, one more mission was added. It was located much farther east and only fifteen miles from the French outpost. It bore the official name of San Miguel de Linares, in honor of the viceroy, the Duke of Linares. It was often called San Miguel de los Adaes, however, the Adaes being a tribe of Indians of the Caddo nation who lived in the vicinity.

The first of the missions to be placed was given the same name as the one abandoned twenty-three years before, San Francisco de los Tejas. In effect it was a re-establishment of the original mission, and the new location was only about ten miles east of the former site. Fittingly, and as an honor to the now highly respected Fray Hidalgo, he was placed in charge of the newly re-born mission. Thus he began once more his ministry to the redskins of eastern Texas.

The mission next most advanced, or nearest to the French, after Los Adaes, was Nuestra Señora de los Dolores de los Ais, in the southern edge of the present day San Augustine, Texas. Mission Nuestra Señora de Guadalupe lay at a site now the corner of North and Mullen Streets, in Nacogdoches, Texas. Mission San José de los Nazonis was built near the present day Cushing, Texas. Five years later San Francisco de los Tejas (sometimes called de los Neches) was moved still again, to a spot west of the present Alto, Texas. The presidio was called Nuestra Señora de los Dolores de los Tejas, and after several moves, was finally located near the present-day Douglass, Texas.

This new effort by the Spaniards was much better planned and organized than previous attempts had been, of course. Nevertheless, enough serious difficulties remained to ensure that life for Hidalgo would not be smooth and uneventful.

The first setback was a strange illness that began to attack the newcomers. One by one the friars, soldiers, and settlers fell sick with a weakening, feverish malady. Fray Hidalgo wrote to his friends back at San Juan Bautista, describing the epidemic. His letter, dated October 6, 1716, has survived and is in the National Archives of Mexico. In it he says that he was one of the first victims, and tells how the sudden sickness hit, and how it lasted from July until mid-October. It was marked by alternate spells when he shook with chills and burned with a high fever. "But now, thanks to God, I am convalescing and have strength to work in the vineyard of the Lord."

Today we can recognize the epidemic as malaria, and as would be expected with this disease, when the approach of winter and cool weather began to thin out the mosquitoes, the scourge subsided. Although winter brought relief from the malaria, it also brought its own hardships.

The season was a severe one for the Spaniards, whose bodies were ill prepared for the biting cold. Blustery "northers" followed one another at intervals of four or five days. Flooding rains, and even occasional snow, made most building and other outside work impossible. Some of the store of corn spoiled, and none of the supplies lasted as long as had been expected.

Most distressing of all for Padre Hidalgo, however, was the behavior of the Indians. While St. Denis was there to handle them, the savages were of some help in building the log chapels and cabins, as well as in the clearing of land for fields and pastures. But the adroit Frenchman soon left to return to San Juan Bautista, and most of the natives lapsed at once into their former way of life.

Although many of the Indians did come in to visit the settlements, it was only to watch in wonder as the white men worked, or to listen in awe and curiosity as the friars celebrated Mass. Few of them could be persuaded to move to the missions, much less to help with the work. Padre Hidalgo traveled great distances through the forests, going from one small village to another, but with all his eloquence, he was able to convert only a handful of the savages and persuade them to submit to the restraints of civilized life with its labor.

A series of disappointments followed one another, and at last the friars despaired of success with the methods they were using. In another long letter, Hidalgo wrote that more soldiers were needed. Only soldiers could handle the Texas Indians, he said. Only with this help could they be won over. The hovels and idols of the savages should be burned by the troopers, he continued, for in this way they could be forced to gather at the missions. "This place is severely lacking of the military." Some of the garrison had deserted and gone back to Mexico, while others were in bed sick. At least a hundred more soldiers would be needed, he thought, to bring the natives firmly under the King of Spain and the Catholic Church.

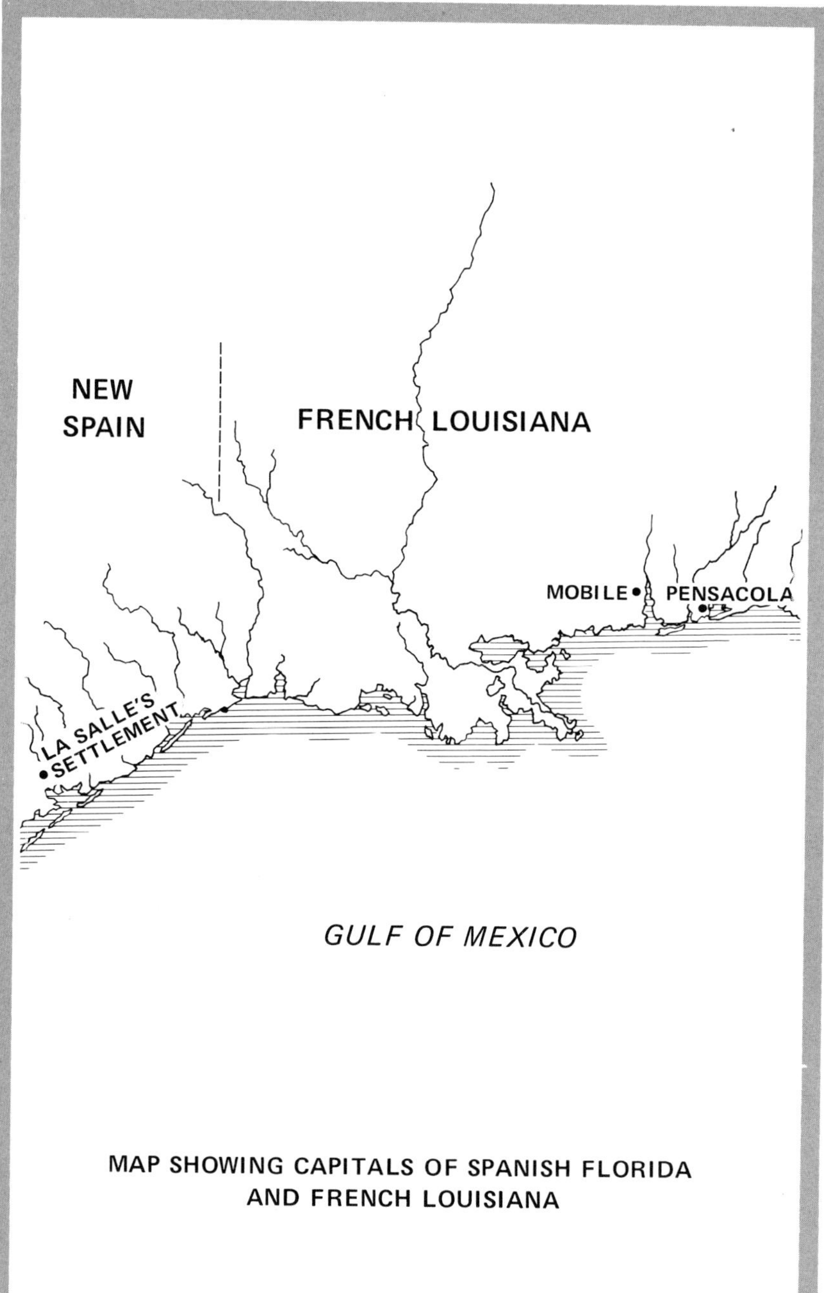

MAP SHOWING CAPITALS OF SPANISH FLORIDA AND FRENCH LOUISIANA

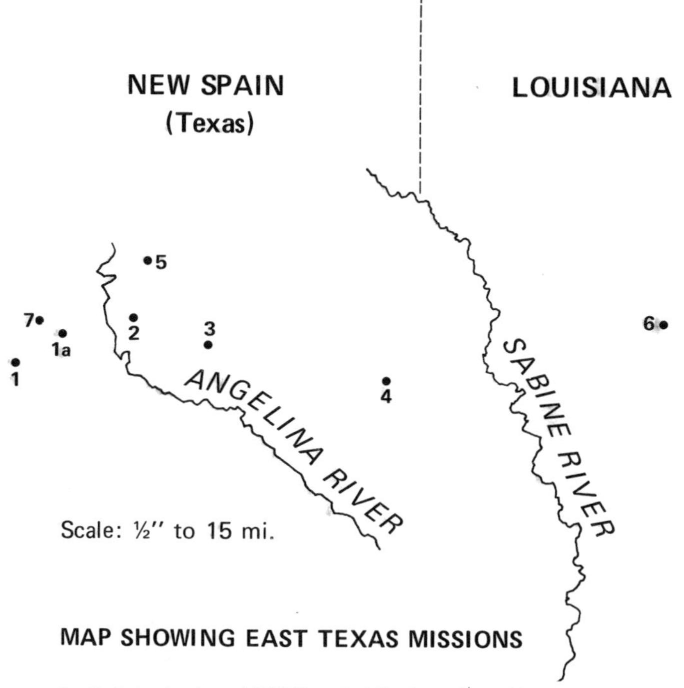

MAP SHOWING EAST TEXAS MISSIONS

1. Original site (1690) of Mission San Francisco de los Tejas (near present-day town of Weches, Texas)

1a. 1716 site of reestablished Mission San Francisco de los Tejas (near Indian Mound, south of present-day Alto, Texas)

2. 1716 site of Mission Nuestra Señora de la Purísima Concepción (near present town of Douglass, Texas)

3. 1716 site of Mission Nuestra Señora de Guadalupe (At North and Mullen Streets in present Nacogdoches, Texas)

4. 1716 site of Mission Nuestra Señora de los Dolores de los Ais (in southern edge of present city of San Augustine, Texas)

5. 1716 site of Mission San Jose de los Nazonis (near present-day Cushing, Texas)

6. 1717 site of Mission San Miguel de Linares, or Adaes (near present-day Robeline, Louisiana)

7. 1721 second site of Mission San Francisco--de los Neches--(six miles west of Alto, Texas)

Turning to the subject of supplies, Hidalgo outlined the shortages, but did not dwell on them. "We have great needs, although God is not failing to meet them. Even in these conflicting wants, already mentioned, we have God until such time as the grandness of His Excellency shall remedy such calamity."

Never overlooking the value of keeping alive the Spanish fear of the French, Hidalgo reported at length on rumors of their activities in Louisiana. The valley of the Mississippi (which the Spanish called the River of the Palisades — Río de las Palisadas) was heavily populated with Indians, he wrote. Traveling by canoe the French traded with those tribes, "and have provided them with guns and many other things in which the French trade."

Closer to the Spanish missions, he went on, the French settlement at Natchitoches was at least three years old, and the French had the Indians firmly under their control. He had heard, he added, that a garrison of more than a hundred soldiers was stationed there.

As Fray Hidalgo no doubt hoped and expected, this letter was sent on to the viceroy. In forwarding it, the guardian at the colegio in Querétaro wrote a note of his own which is short enough to quote in full:

Most Excellent Sir:

As chaplain, although unworthy, of Your Excellency, and loyal vassal of our great monarch, Felipe Quinto (Philip V), God preserve him, I give news to Your Excellency of the state of the extended provinces of Tejas, Cadodashos, Natchitoos, etc., which you will see by the attached writing from one of my religious. I do not doubt that your zeal for defending the Crown of Spain will apply appropriate measures for obstructing the damage threatened by the intervention of the French in those regions. My obligation is to ask God to assist Your Excellency with perfect health and to keep you in all felicity. From this Apostolic College of Your Excellency of the Most Holy Cross of Querétaro, December 29, 1716.

Your least chaplain is at Your Excellency's feet.

Fr. José Diez

The viceroy was impressed by the report, and ordered that preparations be speeded up for building the supporting mission at San Antonio. He also sent four thousand pesos from the royal treasury to the governor of Coahuila and Texas to be used for food and supplies for the distant missions. The governor was busy with other things, however, and put off carrying out the orders. This and a maze of government formalities delayed the relief until after the heavy winter rains came on. By the time the supply train did start out, the rivers were too swollen for it to get across them and reach the far outposts.

The convoy did finally get as far as the Trinity River, but by then it was late January, and the stream was in full flood. Its waters spread out over the bottom land to a width of more than two leagues — five or six miles. After waiting for well over a month for the flood to recede, the friar in charge of the supply train finally gave up. He wrote a letter to Hidalgo and the others telling them that he was leaving the boxes and casks piled in a small grove of trees near the river. This letter he gave to a friendly Indian after exacting from him a promise to take it to its destination as soon as he could get across the river. Having done this, the expedition turned back and started its return to the Río Grande.

Not knowing of these events that were taking place west of the swollen Trinity, Padre Hidalgo and his destitute companions on the frontier could only wonder why their pleas went unanswered. At length Hidalgo sent another appeal, writing that "each day, we find ourselves in greater need of clothing and sustenance. The requirements for celebrating Mass have been used up. I pray that by the time you receive this, you may already have taken action; for, if aid does not come, I fear all will be lost, and with good reason. God grant that you may send a lay religious to bring what may be offered from the Río Grande."

This last appeal did not reach San Juan Bautista until spring. When it did come, the people there thought that the Indian messenger had not kept his promise to take the letter about the supplies to the frontier missions. It was perhaps too much to hope that the poorly concealed piles of boxes and casks in the grove had escaped marauding Indians for a whole winter, and they felt compelled to do something more. So, a hastily organized group of friars and soldiers got together what could be spared at San Juan Bautista and set out on the trail once more.

In east Texas, by this time, the friars and settlers were living on crow meat, field mice, and other small animals that they could catch in traps in the forest. At last, with the coming of spring, the Indian messenger finally reached them with the long delayed letter that had been entrusted to him months before. Smudged and barely legible from handling and weathering, it brought the first notice of what had happened to the supplies.

Like those at San Juan Bautista, Padre Hidalgo and his fellows in east Texas did not dare to hope that the cache had been spared so long. Nevertheless, they got together a little train of pack mules and burros, and sent a party from the settlement to search for the supplies.

By an odd coincidence, the two parties, coming from opposite directions, neared the site of the cache at almost the same time, and met there. To the amazement of all, the entire

The Alamo, originally built to serve as the church of Mission San Antonio de Valero, founded in 1718 by Father Antonio de San Buenaventura y Olivares. Father Francisco Hidalgo succeeded the founder in 1720 and was in charge of this mission until 1724. (*H. L. Summerville photo; courtesy of San José Mission Friary.*)

pile of casks and chests was intact. The provisions were not even damaged by the weather. Only the pack-saddles, which had been placed on top of the pile, had suffered any harm from the winter storms.

This was even more remarkable because the remains of camp fires and other signs showed that a party of Indian buffalo hunters had camped near the grove. Everyone was sure that only by a divine miracle could the supplies have survived. "Heaven favored the cargo," one of them wrote. It had been "in the invisible custody which had hidden for so long the succor of those ministers of God from the eyes of the Indians."

The two groups of old friends had a joyous reunion there in the grove, and offered up many prayers of thanksgiving. Then they had a feast on some of the stored food — to give them strength for their return journeys. After a night of rest, the party from the frontier loaded the strangely blessed supplies on the pack mules and burros. Then they hurried back across the Trinity, to rush the food on with all the speed they could manage toward the needy colonists and missionaries waiting for them in the newly established settlement.

With the arrival of the food and supplies, hope arose once more in the frontier settlement that the newly cleared fields and pastures would yield a harvest before the next winter came on, and everyone set to work with renewed vigor. Fortunately for them, as they labored, they knew nothing of the storm that threatened both them and their homeland in Europe.

16 / War!

With the passing months and years, the struggling missions and settlements in east Texas slowly grew more stable. Nevertheless, Padre Hidalgo still had ample causes for worry in the malaria-plagued wilderness, and these were closer at hand than the far-off rumblings of a coming war in Europe. There was always strife in Europe, and almost always a war. Much more troubling to Hidalgo and his companions were the Indians who stubbornly held to their heathen ways, and inept colonial governments in Mexico City and Monclova. Or at least it seemed so to him and to them.

Along the border between France and Spain, the guns began to thunder in January of 1719. News of the new war did not reach the French colony at Mobile until three months later, however — on April 19th. Holding the post of governor there now was a vigorous man named Jean Baptiste Lemoyne, Sieur de Bienville. When he got word of the war, the governor hurriedly called a meeting of his advisers in the log cabin "capitol," to discuss what should be done. Guessing that the Spanish at nearby Pensacola had not yet heard of the outbreak of war, the French leaders decided to launch an immediate attack on that settlement. This was done, and it resulted in a complete surprise. The unsuspecting Spanish garrison was easily overwhelmed and captured.

At the same time, the French governor sent orders to the

officer in charge at Natchitoches to move against the Spanish who faced him across the border in east Texas. The young commander there, named Blondel, had only a handful of soldiers at Natchitoches, but nevertheless he moved at once against the nearest Spanish mission, just fifteen miles away.

Slipping through the pine forest, the little French force pounced on the enemy outpost. Not only did they succeed in surprising the isolated mission, but found that the friar in charge and most of the others were away on various errands. The mission was manned by one lay brother and one soldier, and of course even they did not know that their country was at war.

Taking the two men prisoners, the French invaders gathered up all the altar ornaments, movable fixtures, and everything else of value that was light enough for them to carry away. Then they turned their attention to the livestock, and especially a small flock of squawking, hard-to-catch chickens which looked quite appetizing.

While the attackers were busy chasing the chickens, the lay brother and the soldier slipped away from them and fled into the forest. As soon as they were sure that they had eluded their pursuers, they turned and hurried toward the other missions farther west, to warn them of the attack. The brother had been in the hands of the French long enough to overhear them talking of the outbreak of war, and of "the intention of the French to drive the Spaniards from Texas." He also heard his captors speaking of a force of a hundred or more soldiers who were on the way to Natchitoches from Mobile to reinforce the French outpost.

Blondel was sure that the escaped prisoners would spread the alarm to the other missions and the presidio garrison. He would no longer have the advantage of surprise, therefore, and since he had only about a squad of men, he decided not to press his little offensive any farther. After all, he already had an impressive victory to report to Governor Bienville, for he had captured a Spanish mission and sacked it. So he returned to Natchitoches, carrying the spoils of his easy conquest.

The Spanish were not aware of Blondel's decision to give up, of course. When the lay brother came in with his story of the attack and the things he had overheard, therefore, it caused a panic. They knew that the force at Natchitoches numbered only a dozen or so soldiers, but it was clear that the Spanish garrison was not nearly strong enough to withstand an assault by the hundred or more reinforcements which were said to be on the way there. Furthermore, the Spanish leaders felt sure that the attackers would be joined by a horde of Indian warriors. The savages were always eager for the warpath, and they were sure to join in an attack by their friends, the French. A massacre seemed certain.

The Spanish officers also knew full well that the viceroy could ill afford to spare soldiers to reinforce them. Even if he could, it would take the reinforcements months to march from Mexico to the Texas border. Because of all this, the shaken Spanish defenders needed little time to decide to fall back to a less exposed and better protected position.

The commander announced the decision and ordered that the retreat begin at daybreak the next morning. Padre Hidalgo was shocked, and protested bitterly, as did some of his fellow missionaries. Their protests were drowned out by the cries of the terrified settlers and the soldiers, however, and preparations began for abandoning the presidio.

It was a cruel turn of events for Hidalgo. Once more he faced having to abandon his mission. Once more he must turn his back on his redskin children and leave them. And if only his pleas for more soldiers had been heeded this would not have happened.

As soon as there was enough light the following morning, the retreat began, friars, settlers, and troopers streaming out with only such food and possessions as they could carry on their backs. By a forced march they put as many leagues behind them that day as they could — between them and the French. Following the trail that ran to San Antonio and on to San Juan Bautista, they hurried over the hills and through the forests of pine.

Three days later the marchers reached the Trinity River. Here the capitán decided that he could safely halt for a time, make camp, and await help. So, while the refugees caught their breaths from the panicky flight, the commander sent frantic appeals for reinforcements to San Antonio and to Mexico.

The viceroy did not have enough troops in New Spain to defend Mexico itself, much less the sprawling outer provinces. Nowhere was there any reserve to draw on to augment the frontier force. This was well known to the ranchers and settlers at San Juan Bautista, and it sharpened the feeling that they ought to respond themselves to the pitiful cries for help that came from the banks of the Trinity. So some of them organized a group of volunteers.

By the time this little force assembled and got together the supplies it needed, however, September had come. Cold weather soon set in and the winter rains began. Now the relief expedition could not get across the soggy prairies and swollen rivers. It did manage to advance a short distance beyond San Antonio, but then had to fall back there to await the return of better conditions.

During all this time, Padre Hidalgo and the rest of the forlorn refugees huddled in their camp on the banks of the

Trinity. No response came to their appeals for help. Their supply of food dwindled rapidly. To add to their discomfort, rumors began to come in to them that somewhere in the forests to the northeast the French were assembling an army of several thousand Indians from several nations. Soon a further rumor spread that the army of Indians had been supplied with horses and guns by the French, and "drilled and given the rudiments of military training." Knowing that they could not defend themselves against such a horde, and with their food running short, the little band of Spaniards once more tied their bundles on their backs and resumed the retreat. Finally reaching San Antonio, they halted once more.

The threats to the colonists were imaginary, of course, and based on mere rumors. Nevertheless, if they had known the truth — all of it — they would have had reason enough to be fearful. For in fact the French king and his courtiers in Paris had now changed their minds about their American empire. Contrary to the former opinion that France already had enough land in that far-off wilderness, they now decided to annex some of the Spanish domain.

Pursuant to this decision, the king of France issued a proclamation declaring that the Río Grande was the true boundary of French Louisiana. He then ordered an invasion of Texas with the aim of taking possession of it and of capturing, at the least, all of the lands east and north of the Río Grande.

This time, however, luck was with the Spanish. It was now their turn to profit from the uncertain communications of the day. The French warship that sailed from its home country bound for Mobile and carrying the royal orders for the campaign against New Spain, ran into a Spanish naval squadron and was captured. Bienville and his French colony in Mobile did not learn of the King's plan to invade and annex Texas until after the end of the war.

17 / *Ebb Tide*

During the winter that followed the flight from east Texas, and until the end of the short war, Fray Hidalgo lived in a hurriedly built stick and mud hut near the walls of the Mission San Antonio de Valero (the Alamo). His hut was but a small protection from the "northers," and the winter was a miserable one for him. He had spent worse ones, however, and his prayers were all for peace — his thoughts were all of the day when he could go back to his post on the frontier.

During those days, as he shivered in his frail hut waiting for the struggle in Europe to end, he would have been happier had he known that it had in reality already ended. The envoys of the warring nations were even then sitting down around a table for lengthy debates on the terms to be written into a peace treaty. The treaty was finally agreed to in February of 1720, but of course news of it did not reach the New World until some months later.

Long before news of peace arrived, a vacancy occurred in the Mission San Antonio de Valero when Fray Olivares, the friar in charge, had to leave. Orders came for Fray Hidalgo to take his place. Supposing that in due time the colegio would send another friar to take over the mission, Hidalgo was glad to have some duties to keep him busy while he waited for the war to end. No replacement came, however, and when in May of 1721 the refugees finally made ready to go back to the abandoned east Texas outposts, Hidalgo had to stand by, sick at heart, watching them march away without him.

Swallowing his bitter disappointment, he turned back to resume the duties of his new post, still hoping that he could soon follow his colleagues to the land of the Tejas. Meanwhile, he sent an urgent plea to his superior in the colegio asking that the new friar for San Antonio de Valero be sent without delay.

As he waited, Hidalgo was gratified to hear that the viceroy had at last ordered additional troops to the east Texas presidio, as he had urged. Adding to his satisfaction, too, was news that St. Denis was being put in charge of the French frontier post at Natchitoches. Although Hidalgo suspected that his old friend and ally might play fast and loose with the Spanish trade laws, he did not mind that. For he was also sure that St. Denis would work for the success of both the Spanish and French colonies on the border.

Hidalgo continued on in the Mission at San Antonio as months stretched out into years. Gradually it became clear to him that there was no intention to send him back to the harsh frontier life on the border with Louisiana. Gradually too, he realized that the reason for this was that younger and more vigorous missionaries were needed there. Nevertheless, he stubbornly refused to admit that it was time for him to retire.

He was unhappy in the relative safety and ease of life in the San Antonio mission. When it dawned on him that he would never be sent back to east Texas, therefore, he began to urge his superiors to let him go out among the wild Apaches who roamed the hills and plains to the north and northwest of San Antonio. These bloodthirsty tribes waged

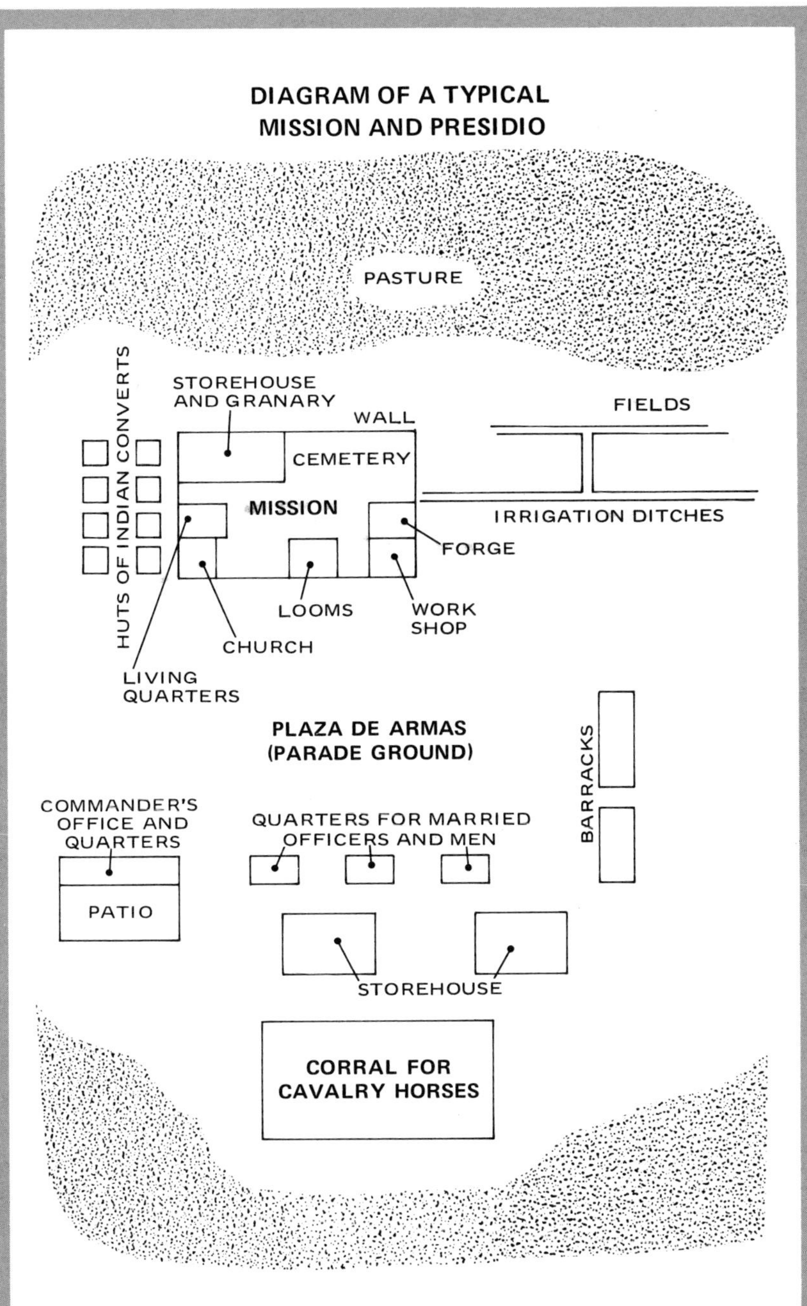
DIAGRAM OF A TYPICAL
MISSION AND PRESIDIO
PASTURE
HUTS OF INDIAN CONVERTS
STOREHOUSE
AND GRANARY
WALL
FIELDS
CEMETERY
MISSION
IRRIGATION DITCHES
FORGE
LOOMS
WORK
SHOP
CHURCH
LIVING
QUARTERS
PLAZA DE ARMAS
(PARADE GROUND)
BARRACKS
COMMANDER'S
OFFICE AND
QUARTERS
QUARTERS FOR MARRIED
OFFICERS AND MEN
PATIO
STOREHOUSE
CORRAL FOR
CAVALRY HORSES

continuous savage warfare against both the whiteskins and all the other Indian tribes within their reach, but Hidalgo insisted that he could tame and convert them.

The Franciscan historian writes of him that during this period, "the Venerable Padre was finding himself already old and oppressed by painful circumstances. Consulting only the robustness of his spirit, however, he began glorious feats with marked vigor. The loving zeal he had for the Apostolic Institute obliged him to ignore the dangers, and to prefer the hope of pacifying those barbarians, and subjecting them to the sacred Laws of the Gospel, to his own life and religious conveniences."

As late as March of 1725, when he was sixty-six years old and his body was broken by the life of hardship and privation he had lived, Hidalgo sent a fervent plea to the presiding friar of the colegio asking for permission to visit the land of the Apaches. He even offered to go without soldiers to protect him. He would, he wrote, "be armed with the sincere desire to take the Gospel to the heathen, and with the hope that peace could be brought to the frontiers."

Although the guardian at this time was Hidalgo's old friend, Friar Pedro Pérez de Mezquía, he could not grant the request. In reply, he wrote to Hidalgo in a gentle and soothing tone, saying that "the flock has been watered with the blood of its pastors many times" but that "the missionaries who content themselves with the fulfillment of the obligations of their charge will find enough to suffer; they could compete, in fact, with the most valiant martyrs, who gave their lives for the Redeemer but once, while these constant ones die innumerable times for their sheep, prepared at all times to shed their blood for them."

In the spring of 1726 orders came to Fray Hidalgo to return to San Juan Bautista, there to retire from active service.

At first, he rebelled against the thought of retiring, but soon realized that he could not avoid obeying the directive. Sad and deeply hurt, but resigned to what could not be avoided, he began the four-day journey over the now well-traveled trail to the Río Grande.

As he plodded along over the familiar countryside, doubtless his thoughts went back across the years to that exciting day in the friary in far off Spain when he first learned that he was chosen to go to the new world — that night when the bright vision came of preaching to the savages in the wilderness. "I was just a boy — only a little past twenty, then," he must have mused. "Now I am sixty-six — a staff that is twisted and broken. But I have lived to triumph. I have seen my vision become a reality — to minister to the pagans — to see many missions among them. God has granted me all this, and I am thankful for it. And He may still have work for me to do."

As he walked, his mind must have pictured his first day in New Spain, that heart-rending day in Veracruz when he stepped ashore into a burning city of dead and dying men. In memory he must have relived the impatient years of waiting for a chance to go to the heathens in the great wilderness beyond the Río Grande. How happy he had been when he finally crossed the great river and went on into the pine forests of east Texas to minister to them and to build a crude log mission in their land.

He could see once more the haunting, wrinkled face of old Totonac as the two men watched the little chapel burn. It had taken many long years of waiting and praying and scheming to do it, but he had at last redeemed his promise to the old chief that he would return to the Tejas.

At last Hidalgo came within sight of the Río Grande and started down into the flood plain and toward the pale green mesquite thickets along the river. Soon the bell tower of Mission San Juan Bautista slowly rose above the brush. He might have muttered, "I will now cross yon river and leave this land as I first entered it, thirty-five long years ago — barefoot and walking, with no worldly goods except my gray robe and my crucifix. Nothing has changed. Yet nothing is the same. My hair is white, my step uncertain, but my spirit is as strong now as it was then. When I shed this stumbling, broken body, I pray God that my freed spirit may once more return and watch over my faltering redskin children."

Back in San Juan Bautista, at the mission he had helped to found, Friar Hidalgo prepared for the end which he now sensed was not far off. With little more to do than celebrating a daily Mass, he had much time to spend in prayer. And there, on November 6, 1726, "his soul was delivered to the Lord."

He was sixty-seven years of age at the time of his death. Since taking the vows of his Order at the age of fifteen, he had lived the life of a mendicant friar for fifty-two years. Forty three of those years he had spent as an apostolic missionary, thirty-five of them in the frontier missions of northern Mexico and Texas.

As he lies today in some unmarked grave in the ruins of Mission San Juan Bautista or the cemetery of the colegio at Querétaro, Padre Francisco Hidalgo deserves a larger place in its pages than History has given him.

Bibliography

Archivo General de la Nación, Mexico, Provincias Internas, Vols. 28, 29, 181, 182. Mexico City. Also in University of Texas Library, Austin.

Arricivita, Juan Domingo. *Crónica Seráfica y Apostólica del Colegio de Propaganda Fide de Santa Cruz de Querétaro en la Nueva España, Segunda Parte,* pages 206, et seq. F. de Zuniga y Ontiveros, Mexico City, 1792.

Canedo, Lino G. *Crónica de los Colegios de Propaganda Fide de la Nueva España,* by Fray Isidro Felix de Espinosa. (New edition with notes and Introduction by Lino G. Canedo O.F.M.). Academy of American Franciscan History, Washington, D.C., 1964.

Carter, Hodding. *Doomed Road of Empire: The Spanish Trail of Conquest,* pages 34, et seq. McGraw Hill Book Co., Inc., New York, 1963.

Castañeda, Carlos E. *Our Catholic Heritage in Texas,* Vol. II. Von Boeckmann-Jones Co., Austin, 1936.

Espinosa, Isidro Felix. (See above, under Canedo.)

Habig, Fr. Marion A., O.F.M. *The Alamo Chain of Missions,* Franciscan Herald Press, Chicago, Ill., 1968; and authorities cited therein.

Phares, Ross. *Cavalier in the Wilderness: The Story of the Explorer and Trader, Louis Juchereau de St. Denis.* Louisiana State University Press, Baton Rouge, 1952.

Robles, Vito Alessio. *Coahuila y Tejas en la Época Colonial,* pages 474, et seq. Editorial Cultura, Mexico City, 1938.

Weddle, Robert S. *San Juan Bautista, Gateway to Spanish Texas.* University of Texas Press, Austin, 1968.

APPENDIX

Letters of Fr. Hidalgo

Although this book tells the life-story of Fr. Hidalgo in a popular rather than a scholarly way, special care has been taken to make it historically accurate. For historians and others as well, it was thought, the value of this biography would be enhanced by the addition of an appendix containing an English translation of eight letters of Fr. Hidalgo, of which copies have been assembled in the Old Spanish Missions Historical Research Library at San José Mission (abbreviated RLSJ), in San Antonio, Texas. The translations were made by Fr. Benedict Leutenegger O.F.M. with the help of Miss Elena Tovar; and the introductions and notes were contributed by Fr. Marion A. Habig O.F.M.

---

1. Letter of May 17, 1704

Addressed to the Father Guardian (superior) of the College of Santa Cruz in Querétaro, Mexico, namely Fr. José Diez (1703-1706), this letter of the three members of the College who were the missionaries of the three missions in Coahuila near the Rio Grande make two requests. The missionaries were: Fr. Joseph García, who at this time was the Father President of the College's missions in Coahuila; Fr. Francisco Hidalgo, who had returned to the San Juan Bautista missions after serving one term as Father Guardian of the College (1701-1703); and Fr. Antonio de San Buenaventura y Olivares, who with Fr. Hidalgo, had founded San Juan Bautista and San Francisco Solano missions in 1700. The third mission, San Bernardo, was founded in 1702. All three missions were at first near present Guerrero, Coahuila, Mexico, where the Presidio of San Juan Bautista was established in 1703. In the same year, Fr. Olivares moved San Francisco Solano Mission sixteen leagues to the west. The original Spanish letter is in the Archives of the College of Querétaro (ACQ), which are now in Celaya, Mexico; and a microfilm copy and a print made from it are in RLSJ.

Very Rev. Father:

We have conferred among the Reverend Ministers of these missions on the subject of how useful and necessary storehouses are to take care of the souls who are at present being instructed and catechized, and to attract the many souls who come to ask for ministers. We see also that these ministers are in urgent need, and some churches are in not a little poverty. It has been decided, therefore, that a religious should go to see Your Reverence to decide and dispose what is most pleasing to God and in conformity with our apostolic institute concerning the following points:

First, we ask Your Reverence to accompany the Reverend Father who is to go and ask His High Excellency the Viceroy to grant kindly the storehouses for the four established missions[1] and another one for the mission that is beyond them.

Secondly, that in regard to our needs, Your Reverence, decide on one of these things, either to ask for the full alms which usually are given to the missionaries, or a portion which should be sufficient for the churches and for the needs of the religious,[2] or that Your Reverence assume the obligation to assist apostolically in all the needs, and that the missionaries say Mass for the intention of Your Reverence just as the Reverend Fathers do who live in the holy College.[3] This is what we ask of Your Reverence, all of us, the undersigned.

May 17, 1704.

Fr. Joseph García (rubric)
Fr. Francisco Hidalgo (rubric)
Fr. Antonio de S. Buena y Olivares (rubric)

---

1. The fourth mission of the College of Querétaro at this time was Mission Santa Maria de los Dolores, at Lampazos, Nuevo León, about a hundred miles south of Guerrero, Coahuila; it was founded in 1689. "The mission that is beyond them" was probably Mission San Bernardino de la Candela or Caldera, in Coahuila, about twenty miles southwest of Lampazos, founded about 1687, by Fr. Damian Mazanet, as Mission Santiago del Valle de Candela, and surrendered to the care of the Franciscan Province of Jalisco in 1690. Cf. Fr. I. F. de Espinosa, *Crónica,* ed. by L. G. Canedo (Washington, D. C., 1964), pp. 671 and 675, note 3; also R. S. Weddle, *San Juan Bautista* (Austin: Univ. of Texas Press, 1968), p. 20.

2. The government usually allotted to each of the missionaries on the frontier an annual allowance of 450 pesos for his personal needs. It is suggested here that the College accept this allowance, or a part of it, as an alms with which it would be possible to purchase what the missions and the missionaries needed. The friars at the College did not handle the funds themselves. This was done by a layman, called an "apostolic syndic."

2. Letter of September 8, 1706

Fr. Joseph García has returned to the College of Querétaro, and Fr. Hidalgo has succeeded him as Father President of the San Juan Bautista missions. Besides Fr. Olivares, he now has two new missionaries as companions, Fr. Cervantes and Fr. Espinosa. Fr. Hidalgo and his fellow missionaries write to the viceroy, thanking him for granting the annual allowance of 450 pesos for each of the missionaries. But, as Franciscans who had no possessions of their own, they renounce the allowance for personal use and ask that it be regarded as an alms for the needs of their missions. The paragraphing of the letter is the editor's. The original Spanish letter is in ACQ; and a microfilm copy and print from the latter are in RLSJ.

Most Excellent Lord:

Fr. Francisco Hidalgo of the Seraphic Order of our Father St. Francis, apostolic preacher, ex-guardian of the College of Santa Cruz de Querétaro, and at present the president of the missions of the Propagation of the Faith of the Rio Grande of the North, the boundary of the province of Coaguila, and the other religious laboring in those missions, come before Your Excellency in due form and according to the law, and say that since Fr. Preacher, Fr. Joseph García, who was president of those missions, has sent a report to Your Excellency, it is to be noted that a great number of gentiles has been taken from these lands in order to nourish the converts, because of the sterility of the lands, the lack of harvest, and also the inability of the Indians to be educated.[4]

---

3. The alternative suggested is that the College would take care of the needs of the missions and missionaries by using funds supplied by private benefactors, especially those who gave an offering or stipend when they requested that one or more holy Masses be celebrated for their intention or intentions. The missionaries would offer up the holy Masses, and the stipends would be retained by the College to buy what was needed in the missions.

4. The meaning seems to be, that the number of pagan Indians gathered at the missions was reduced by letting some of them go back to their haunts, because it was not possible to feed them all at the mission. Thus, when San Bernardo was founded in 1702, no less than 400 Indians had been gathered in the mission by May of that year; but in 1727, when this mission was well established, the total number of Indians living in it was only one half of the original number. Cf. R. S. Weddle, *op. cit.*, pp. 53 and 175.

This is the reason why I asked and do ask Your Excellency to grant warehouses to make progress and to preserve most securely the converts; also that by way of alms and without the title for allowance, some emolument be set aside for them; others (alms) also should be made for the churches of said missions.

We are aware of the goodness of Your Excellency, who with the general council provided favorably, for those missions and for their laborers, a remedy in their needs, which said Father mentioned should be granted for each year (a testimony of the prompt assistance of the ministers), the amount of 450 pesos for each minister; these are to be distributed for their needs as expressed, and the money is to be taken from the royal treasury in the city of San Luis Potosí.[5]

What has been presented is as Father said, and the needs which the ministers feel are many; but we are conscious of the most pure observance of our apostolic institute, as also of the necessary expenses incurred by our Catholic Monarch with the pleas coming from so many wars; therefore, for the present, and as far as it pertains to us, we renounce and give up said alms, once, twice, and three times, and all which by right can be acquired.

We are content with what the goodness of Your Excellency should grant us only for the Indians, for thus will be supplied the plows and other implements needed for cultivating the soil; the Indians will then be induced to work on the farms; they will be ready and more eager for the Christian and civilized way of life, until so much is gained that His Majesty, our King and Lord, need not undergo more expenses from the royal treasury. This seems good to us for the service of both Majesties. This is all I can say at present.

Mission of San Juan Baptista, September 8, 1706.

Your most humble chaplains kiss the feet of Your Excellency.

Fr. Francisco Hidalgo
(rubric)
President and Commissary
of the Missions

Fr. Anto de S. Buenta
(rubric)

Fr. Diego Xavier Cervantes
(rubric)

Fray Isidro de Espinosa
(rubric)

3. *Letter of October 9, 1706*

The contents of this letter, addressed to the superiors of the College of Querétaro, are similar to those of the preceding letter to the viceroy. The superiors are called "Presidente in Capite and the Discreets" or Councillors, because the term of office of Fr. Guardian José Diez (1703-1706) had just expired and the missionaries on the Rio Grande had not yet learned who the newly elected Father Guaridan was. Actually, as they found out later, it was Fr. Olivares, one of those who signed the letter. The Presidente in Capite took Fr. Olivares' place until he arrived at Querétaro; and Fr. Olivares served as guardian until 1709. The letters "J.M.J." at the beginning of the letter are an abbreviation of "Jesus, Mary, Joseph." The original Spanish letter is in ACQ; and a microfilm copy and a print of the latter is in RLSJ.

J.M.J.

Most Rev. Fathers, our brothers, the Presidente in Capite, and the Discreets of our holy College:

Fray Francisco Hidalgo of the Order of our holy Father St. Francis, apostolic preacher, ex-guardian and present president of these missions of the Rio Grande del Norte, and all the religious who have signed below, we come before Your Reverences to say that His High Excellency the Viceroy has assigned someone to distribute alms for the missions of 450 pesos for each missionary (as Your Reverences know).

We realize that it is more fitting for our apostolic institute, and it is more closely related to our profession and more in harmony with the mind of the religious of our College, to make the total renunciation (in as far as matters pertain to us) of said alms. We come before Your Reverences once, twice, and three times, and assert our wish to appear as poor evangelists and as sons (though unworthy) of the Father of the poor, who has not forgotten (as we hope) those who come beneath his shadow.

Likewise, we are encouraged to rely upon the solicitude of this holy Seminary, which, we do not doubt, will provide a religious,

5. Because of the renunciation made by the missionaries, the royal treasury in San Luis Potosi did not pay out the allowance of 450 pesos to the missionaries themselves but to the "apostolic syndic" of the College of Querétaro; and, with these "alms," supplies were purchased and sent to the missions.

who has the necessary qualifications to look after the appropriate alms needed to make progress and to obtain for us the habit and religious sustenance; in this way the needs will be met and the religious who serve (the missions) and will serve (them) in the future, will take courage.

To obtain these alms from the King our Lord, for whom we wish happiness, we shall be in some way obliged to serve the missions, and if at some time the holy College gives them up (as can happen for just reasons), they will acquaint us with what is needed and of the expenses of the royal treasury; in the renunciation made under the Lord Viceroy, the Fathers will see more clearly our intent. If the Ven. Discretorio will deem it agreeable, it can present this renunciation to His Excellency; and if not, that will be the most fitting what the Rev. Fathers decide.

Furthermore, if the Lord of the vineyard provides ministers, a way will be open to go to vast regions of infidels, which each day (not without tears) we see. This work is hindered because of the lack of alms from His Majesty, for by not getting alms the ministers are reduced.

Finally, we shall be pleased when these missions make adjustments in the alms with their head, the holy College. We hope that the disadvantage of these missions in being so remote from places of recourse will be overcome by the love of our dear brothers of this College, who will take the most appropriate measures; those whom profession made brothers, our apostolic institute brought together in unity in remedying their needs and in the manner in which the College passes on the alms from benefactors to these missions. All of us are at the feet of Your Reverences, whose lives may heaven bless.

From these missions of the Rio Grande del Norte, October 9, 1706.

The holy and venerable Discretorio, your least brothers and servants kiss the feet of Your Reverences.

Fr. Francisco Hidalgo
(rubric)
President and Commissary
of the Missions

Fr. Antonio de S. Buenta
(rubric)

Fr. Diego Xavier Cervantes
(rubric)

Fr. Isidro de Espinosa
(rubric)

4. *Letter of July 22, 1716*

In this letter to the viceroy, the nine priest missionaries in eastern Texas briefly report the founding of the first four of the six missions which were to be established there as a joint project of the two Franciscan Missionary Colleges of Querétaro and Zacatecas. Of the nine priests, whose signatures appear at the end, besides Fr. Espinosa and Fr. Hidalgo, Frs. Gabriel Vergara, Benito Sánchez, and Manuel Castellanos belonged to the College of Querétaro; the other four were members of the College of Zacatecas. Another Querétaran friar who went along with the Ramón expedition, Fr. Pedro de Mezquia, did not remain in eastern Texas. Besides the nine priests, there were three Franciscan brothers in eastern Texas at this time: Brothers Francisco Xavier Cubillos, Francisco de San Diego, and Domingo de Urioste, the last one mentioned being a *donado,* or Third Order brother. Fr. Margil and his two companions, who could not go with Ramón because of Margil's illness, had reached eastern Texas before July 22.

The four missions founded to date were: the second Mission San Francisco de los Tejas, on July 5, near present Alto, with Fr. Hidalgo as missionary and Fr. Castellanos as companion and chaplain of the presidio; Mission Nuestra Señora de la Purísima Concepción, on July 6, six miles south of present Douglass; Nuestra Señora de Guadalupe, on July 9, in present Nacogdoches; and San José de los Nazonis, on July 10, two and a half miles north of present Cushing. The first two and the fourth were in the care of the College of Querétaro. The Nacogdoches mission was founded in the absence of Fr. President Margil; and subsequently he founded two more in accordance with the division line mentioned farther on in the letter.

The original report as well as the attestation which follows it are in the Archivo General y Publico de la Nacion (AGN), Historia, vol. 27, Mexico City. Copies of both are in ACZ; and microfilm copies of the latter are in RLSJ.

A Report Made to His Excellency by the Reverend Fathers Missionaries

Most Excellent Sir:

By the will of His Divine Majesty, after a two months' journey from the Rio Grande del Norte to this beautiful province of Asinay or Texas, we succeeded in establishing four missions: the first one is under the patronage of our Father San Francisco, restoring the ancient pueblo four leagues farther in an easterly direction; it includes the Nascha, Nabeitdacho and Nacachas

Nations. The second mission is La Purísma Concepción, eight leagues from the first, with the Asinay Indians and is well populated. The third mission was dedicated to Our Lady of Guadalupe, another eight leagues farther to the southeast, with the Nocodochis Indians, and this mission is also well populated. All three are on the road to the Nachitos, where on several occasions those men of the new French nation and Palizada[6] have penetrated. The fourth mission is to the northeast, about seven leagues from Mission Concepción and was called San Joseph. The main mission of those about to be founded by the College of Zacatecas is the one of Our Lady of Guadalupe. The arrival of natives of the same language and culture is expected and their settlement will take place shortly.

We have fostered great hopes, Most Excellent Lord, that this province will be a new Philippine,[7] having in the first place the protection of Your Excellency. The Indians have welcomed us with great friendliness. This, we recognize, deserves the gentleness and kind attitude which the Catholic magnificence of our King and Lord (may God preserve him) should show them as sons of his love and extend his goodness by joining hands with us to cover their nakedness, to cultivate their lands, and to raise cattle for their sustenance. It is our obligation to assure the just distribution of whatever is given them, and as we recognize the special need of each one, more adequate help will be given.

We leave to the supreme understanding of Your Excellency what is in itself obvious in regard to divine worship and the precise needs of the religious. At a distance of more than 300 leagues from the nearest settlements, recourse cannot be had to our benefactors, nor is there any reason to expect alms, nor can increased expenses and well known native dangers be avoided. We are notifying our superiors on this point so that they may make this especially clear to the paternal providence of Your Excellency, from whom we await full relief.

---

6. The "Nachitos" Indians were at the present Natchitoches, Louisiana; and the Palizada was the Mississippi River.

7. Throughout the eighteenth century not a few official documents used the name "Provincia de Texas o de Nuevas Filipinas" — the Province of Texas or the New Philippines.

We bring to the notice of Your Excellency that the land of the infidels has been divided between the Colleges of the Propagation of the Faith of the Holy Cross of Querétaro and of Our Lady of Guadalupe of Zacatecas in this way: the College of the Holy Cross directs its conversions from the east to the north and west in that part of the country that runs in a straight line to the Cadodachos and can in the course of time reach New Mexico; the College of Zacatecas directs its efforts along the line from the east to the south and from there to the west until it meets Tampico and the populated area in that direction. According to delayed information recently acquired, grain harvest is most abundant on both sides, and the nations are large, though far from us at present.

All this land is thought to be rich in minerals, as experts tell us, though they have not been found as yet, nor have tests been made; but their discovery will facilitate the settlement by inhabitants, who, we most earnestly pray, will be orderly in conduct, and that no one will be forced, nor found to be in evil ways, because good or bad habits and actions are passed on unconsciously from our people to those of this land.

Since we are aware of the many occupations of Your Excellency, a more detailed report of this territory and of its inhabitants is not included. The daily report[8] has been divided, in case Your Excellency would like to review it, when you are not so busy, in order to get some idea of what this delayed conversion promises. May the Lord extend the years of Your Excellency and give you every success.

Mission of Purísima Concepción, July 22, 1716.

At the feet of Your Excellency, your most humble chaplains

Fr. Antonio Margil de Jesús,
President of the Missions of Zacatecas

Fr. Isidro Felix de Espinosa,
President of the Missions of Santa Cruz de Querétaro

---

8. The "daily report" sent to the viceroy was no doubt the *Diario derrotero . . . Año de 1716* of Fr. Espinosa (AGN, Provincias Internas, vol. 181, part 1, pp. 95-121), of which an English translation by Gabriel Tous has been published in *Texas Catholic Historical Society Preliminary Studies,* I, no. 4 (Austin, 1930), under the title: *Ramón's Expedition: Espinosa's Diary of 1716.*

Fr. Matías Saens de San Antonio
Fr. Francisco Hidalgo
Fr. Pedro de Santa Maria y Mendoza
Fr. Gabriel Vergara
Fr. Agustín Patrón
Fr. Benito Sanchez
Fr. Manuel Castellano

Attestation of the Reverend Missionary Fathers

All the undersigned presidents of the two colleges of Santa Cruz de Querétaro and of Nuestra Señora de Guadalupe de Zacatecas with the religious who are assisting in these missions of the province of Nuestro Padre San Francisco de los Asinay (popularly known as Texas), we do certify to Your Excellency, the Lord Duke of Linares, Viceroy of this New Spain, in the best form possible, that all that is mentioned in the preceding report is the truth on which we have agreed both as to the journey to this province and also as to the time we have labored in these new missions. We hope from the Christian charity of Your Excellency that you will make provisions in accord with your ardent zeal for the greatest spread of our holy Catholic Faith and the extension of the royal Crown. This your least chaplains ask of Your Excellency.[9]

Fray Antonio Margil de Jesús,
President of the Missionaries of the College of Zacatecas
Fray Isidro Feliz de Espinosa,
President of the Missionaries of Santa Cruz de Querétaro
Fray Matías Saenz de San Antonio
Fray Francisco Hidalgo
Fray Pedro Santa María de Mendoza
Fray Benito Sánchez
Fray Agustín Patrón
Fray Manuel Castellanos
Fray Gabriel Vergara

---

9. The attestation has no date, but it does have the same signatures as the foregoing report, although not in the same order. Very probably it was added to this report and the *Diario* of Fr. Espinosa, when both were sent to the viceroy.

5. *Letter of October 6, 1716*

Fr. Hidalgo and his companion at Mission San Francisco de los Tejas, Fr. Castellanos, write a long and important letter to Fr. Pedro de Mezquía, the Father President of the San Juan Bautista missions (as is indicated by the words "Very Reverend"), with the request that it be passed on to Fr. Diego de Salazar (perhaps at Lampazos) and by him forwarded to the viceroy. Fr. Hidalgo mentions that he suffered from fevers and chills from July to October; states that only four missions had been founded thus far; relates that missionaries from other missions, including Fr. Margil from Nacogdoches, came to celebrate the feast of St. Francis (October 4) at Mission San Francisco; and refers to a trip that Captain Ramón made to Natchitoches during the summer.

All this makes it clear that the second and third Zacatecan missions were not founded during the summer of 1716. In his letter of February 13, 1718 (cf. *El Campanario,* March, 1971, p. 2) Fr. Margil writes that these missions were founded when he accompanied Ramón on a subsequent trip to Natchitoches. The second Zacatecan mission to be founded was that of San Miguel de los Adaes, near present Robeline, Louisiana, only about fifteen miles southwest of Natchitoches. And on the way back, near San Augustine, Texas, the third mission, Nuestra Señora de los Dolores was founded. Fr. Margil (writing in 1718) does not report that the trip was made and the missions were established in the fall of 1716; and so Fr. Espinosa, in his *Crónica* (Fr. Lino Canedo's edition, 1964, p. 724), may be correct after all when he writes that the Dolores and San Miguel missions were founded during the first months of 1717, though he is mistaken when he says they were founded in that order.

Fr. Pedro de Mezquía to whom the letter is addressed accompanied the Ramón expedition to eastern Texas in 1716, and then returned to San Juan Bautista. He also went along with Governor Alarcón's expedition in 1718, for the founding of the San Antonio mission, presidio, and villa in May, and to eastern Texas in the fall; and he wrote a diary of this expedition. Later he twice served as Father Guardian of the College of Querétaro (1724-1727 and 1730-1733).

The original Spanish letter is in the Biblioteca Nacional, Mexico City; a microfilm copy is at the Academy of American Franciscan History, Washington, D. C.; and a transcript made from the latter is in RLSJ.

Very Reverend Father Pedro Mezquía:

Long live Jesus! I have informed Your Reverence that I and

Fr. Manuel Castellano are now the ministers of the first Mission of our holy Father St. Francis. I am in charge of the Indians and Father is chaplain of the presidio, which is some four leagues from the mission. Both of us have been ill; I was one of the first to succumb and was ill from the month of July until a few days ago, but thanks be to God, I am now feeling better and can work in the vineyard of the Lord. Fr. Manuel took sick much later but God willed that he should get better and is now much improved. The sickness was marked by spells of fever and chills.

With this explanation I reckon that His Excellency will not find fault with us for not writing and sending letters with the mail that has been going out. Four missions have been founded; the first one is the Mission of San Francisco for the Indians of the Nabeidacho, Neicha, Nacachao, and Nacono tribes. As yet they have not come to live at the mission, though some effort to bring this about has been made. God will provide that more soldiers will come and bring help, for at present the number of soldiers is low; some have fled and others are sick in bed.

The Indians adore false gods; they have houses of worship and keep a perpetual fire burning in the house of the main idol. Some Indians have accepted the Faith and on the feast day of our Father St. Francis, many Indian men and women from different sections of the country assisted at the High Mass. Fr. President came from Mission Concepción and Fr. Benito Sanches came from Mission San Joseph, where the Indians of the Nazoni and Nadacao tribes live. Fr. Antonio Margil came from Mission Nuestra Señora de Guadalupe, where the Nacogdoches and Nacaos Indians are assembled.

As yet religious instructions have not been started with the Indians, and one reason is that their homes are so widely scattered. Little by little we are trying to get them to live where we live, and with God's help a start will be made soon. Another reason for delaying instructions is that if we try to have them give up their idols and temples and burn them, and become subjects of the King and of the Church, one hundred soldiers will be needed. This is a small number, since the nation is increasing and a greater number of natives live farther inland.

The French are trying to settle the Nazoni, Nacitos, Nadedos, and Naquise tribes farther south, some 40 leagues down the river from the Cadodachos Indians. The Captain was there; now the Nachittos are on an island in the river, settled three years ago by two Frenchmen, who are keeping the Indians firmly in subjection. They are awaiting one hundred soldiers from Mobile to settle the place with a show of force. Nevertheless, the Captain came with his staff of command and the royal insignia and ordered the French to erect a cross which he had them make; an altar was put up and Mass was said, and I reckon the Kings will discuss the question of indemnity.

The Nachitos Indians are numerous and have taken over other sections of the country, in which the Asinay Indians, a very large nation, live. All these Indians are Tejas Indians, and from the first mission to the last mentioned tribe of the Nachitoch, the distance is 92 leagues, as Captain Domingo Ramón stated in his diary.

We are in great need but God will not fail to give us what we need so badly in the trying conditions just referred to. God will sustain us until the generosity of His Excellency brings relief to our misery. I am glad I can give this letter to my very dear Father Diego de Salazar, who will forward it to His Excellency. Meanwhile, the Captain is gathering all available information about the French and how they are settling in Mobile and along the Palizada,[10] where Diego Ramón, the brother of the Captain, went to reconnoiter, since Captain Domingo Ramón was ill at that time. This will help to bring it about that His Excellency will gather more supplies and send more soldiers, as this nation is increasing rapidly.

Farther inland more Frenchmen are found, so that it is necessary to investigate and prevent them from crossing the Misuri River, which flows more than 100 leagues farther inland from the Cadodachos River.[11] So the Frenchmen have told me, though the two Frenchmen told Captain Domingo Ramón that it was more than 300 leagues away. What is certain is that the distance is a little more than 100 leagues. This Misuri River empties into the Palizada; both are large rivers and so one's attention is drawn to

10. The Mississippi River.

11. The Misuri is the Missouri River, and the Cadodachos is the Red River.

the west.[12]

Where the rivers join, the French have settled and have two missions under the care of French Jesuits.[13] They intend to place French missionaries among the Caymo Indians, who, the French say, number five thousand. This tribe is 100 leagues up the Misuri River. The French missionaries are wanted also for the Pani tribe, 50 leagues farther up stream, where the three branches of the river unite to form a very large river. Here French canoes do business with these Indian tribes and provide them with guns and other articles. In the middle stream a few Frenchmen found a large city inhabited by another tribe that is very civilized and well dressed. Don Luis[14] is of the opinion that when he left Mobile 150 Frenchmen set out to explore the place. There is great need to await further information from Mobile. Finally, this is enough to make our great Monarch become concerned about his possessions.

May it please God to grant all the Fathers the best of health that we can wish for you. From our hearts we kiss your hands. October 6, 1716.

Fr. Francisco Hidalgo
Fr. Manuel Castellano

---

6. Letter of April 18, 1718

Fr. Hidalgo writes a letter to the viceroy in behalf of his friend, Louis Juchereau de St. Denis. Making a second attempt to start com-

---

12. As early as 1714, the Sieur Vensard de Bourgmond navigated the Missouri River as far as its junction with the Platte River (cf. J. Rothensteiner, *History of the Archdiocese of St. Louis,* St. Louis, 1928, I, 50).

13. These two missions, near the confluence of the Missouri and the Mississippi, were Holy Family Mission at Cahokia, Illinois, opposite St. Louis, founded in 1700 by Father John Bergier, a priest of the Seminary of Quebec, and taken over by the Jesuits at his death in 1712; and the Kaskaskia Mission, situated since 1703 and 1705 in present Randolph County, Illinois, at the mouth of the Okaw or Kaskaskia River, which flowed into the Mississippi (cf. *ibid.,* pp. 51-54 and 65 ff). Later, because of a change in the river's course, Kaskaskia became an island.

14. Louis Juchereau de St. Denis, who served as "conductor of supplies" in the Ramón expedition to eastern Texas. Cf. C. E. Casteñeda, *Our Catholic Heritage in Texas,* II, 38.

mercial relations between the French and the Spaniards, St. Denis, who was now the husband of the granddaughter of Captain Diego Ramón, Sr., of San Juan Bautista, arrived in Mexico City for the second time in June, 1717, was imprisoned, then released with orders not to leave, but escaped from Mexico City. Fr. Hidalgo may have learned that St. Denis had been cast into prison. He asks the viceroy to send St. Denis, with his wife, back to eastern Texas for the good of the missions. The original Spanish of this letter is in the Archivo de Indias, Seville, Spain; a microfilm copy is in the Stephen F. Austin State University Library, Nacogdoches, Texas, and a copy of the latter in RLSJ.

Most Excellent Lord:

Taking for granted that the news has reached Your Excellency of the state of this province and of the needs that the religious and the soldiers are experiencing, I cannot omit as a Catholic to mention the greatest need that the Indians are suffering in their souls, which with singular evidence I have observed, after the report which the Rev. Fathers and the Captain have presented to Your Excellency.

During the time the mail has been held up in this Mission of San Francisco, which has been now for 56 days, without knowing as yet when it shall go out, the Indians have been and are in great numbers dying without holy baptism, since they are scattered and live from each other at a great distance, and rivers and streams run through the middle, which during the rains, as has happened now, flood to such a stage that no human forces can ford them.

To try to unite these people is so necessary that without it no progress can be made to reach the main goal, for which Your Excellency in the name of His Majesty has sent us, and that is, to plant the Faith among the gentiles. This is above all the greatest need, and a remedy, most urgent and efficacious, will be for Your Excellency to send to this province, with whatever title, Captain Don Luis de San Denis, a Frenchman, for whom these Indians have a special affection. They promised him to assemble when he should come with his wife. I find no difficulty in this, since he is a man of good blood, a subject of our King and very loyal, married to a Spanish woman, and far removed from all bartering. This is as much as I can bring, as of now, before Your

Excellency. May the Divine Majesty preserve your person for His glory, the increase of the holy Faith and of the royal Crown.

Mission of San Francisco de los Texas, April 18, 1718.

Your least chaplain and humble servant kisses the feet of Your Excellency.

Fr. Francisco Hidalgo

---

7. Letter of November 3, 1723

In the summer of 1719, because of a war between France and Spain, Fr. Hidalgo had to retreat with the other Spaniards from eastern Texas, and in the fall began to reside at Mission San Antonio de Valero, which had been founded by Fr. Olivares on May 1, 1718. There he and others waited for the Aguayo expedition, which re-established the six missions in eastern Texas in 1721. Meanwhile, however, Fr. Hidalgo had received another appointment. On September 8, 1720, by order of Fr. Diego de Alcantara, the Father Guardian of the College of Querétaro (1719-1721), Fr. Hidalgo succeeded Fr. Olivares as the missionary in charge of Mission San Antonio.

Some three years later, Fr. Hidalgo sent to the next Father Guardian, who was none other than Fr. Espinosa (1722-1724), his longest letter, a detailed account of the efforts made by his assistant and companion, Fr. Joseph González, to establish peaceful relations with the Apaches, and of this missionary's disagreements with Captain Nicolas Flores, the commander of the Presidio de San Antonio. Fr. González, it seems, misinterpreted the Captain's caution as being opposition to his plans for peace and missionary work among the Apaches. The Captain was removed from office but, after receiving favorable testimonials from Fr. Margil and Fr. Miguel Núñez de Haro of Mission San José in 1724, was reinstated. Fr. González was recalled in 1727 and lost his life while traveling from San Antonio to the Rio Grande.

The original Spanish letter is in ACQ, Celaya, Mexico; and a microfilm copy and print from the latter is in RLSJ.

Rev. Fr. Guardian:

Long live Jesus and his most sorrowful Mother Mary, our Lady. May they be in the heart of Your Reverence and fill your soul with love and happiness. It will give me great pleasure if Your Reverence is in perfect health and in the joy of the Holy Spirit together with that holy community. That which I enjoy is, thanks be to God our Lord, the opportunity to serve Your Paternity in all that you may command.

I must share with Your Reverence the news of the successful undertaking, which God has granted us of having gained the pacification of the Apache Nation. Your Reverence will become acquainted with this by putting down the conditions and means, which are as follows:

The situation was this: the Indians of that nation ran away with half of the horses because they were so poorly guarded. Fr. Joseph Gonzales raised his voice among some of the soldiers, saying that it was a good time for a squadron of soldiers to go out with a group of friendly people from the mission to get the horses back in the same way that they would do it over here without causing any harm, so as not to stir up the hornet's nest and to run the risk of having the settlement razed to the ground, because of the weak defense of the presidio to resist the ferocity of a nation so large and warlike as it is.

These words of Father reached the Captain's ear and he decided to come with his soldiers to consult if it would be opportune to pursue the enemy. Fr. Joseph Gonzales replied that it would not be advisable to strike a blow, so as not to agitate the settlement even more; that the only proper and inexcusable thing to do would be to go with 30 men and the friendly people of this mission to get the horses without the enemy knowing it. This suggestion was accepted and carried out.

They set out with the number of men already mentioned on August 27 and reached a place where they could send out spies. This was done and the spies returned with the information that they reached the site where the Apaches were encamped when they stole the horses. There they had divided the horses among five squadrons. These then separated in groups, each one taking a different route. The spies followed one of these squadrons, having come upon it by chance, for it turned out that it was impossible for them not to come upon it.

Having withdrawn from the soldiers and the friendly people, the thieves, about 50 Indians, took to flight; some were killed from the back as they fled down a wooded creek, and 20 women and some boys were captured on the day of Our Lady of Mercy, September 24. They then started the return trip with said captives, and at the end of two days' journey, the Captain sent a messenger to bring the news of the events. He informed Fr. Gonzales that among the captives was an Indian woman of competent age who could be sent to ask for peace from her companions.

Father wrote immediately to Captain Nicolas Flores that it would serve both Majesties if he without delay would send the Indian woman, and act in the best possible way so that she would speak with her companions and let them know our good intention of not harming them if they became our friends; if they did not accept the offer, he would proceed to carry out the just punishment against them as rebels. But the captain made no move and paid no attention to my opinion, which I thought so holy, just, and fitting. He finally reached this presidio on October 9.

For the second time Father urged that it was imperative to send the Apache woman but the Captain did not agree. He proceeded without making any agreement or attending to the cause of God and of the king to distribute the captives among the soldiers, as is customary. Lieutenant Diego Ramón was ready to set forth with his and the soldiers' share of the captives. Father heard of this and urged for the third time to consider the surrendering of that Indian woman, who was being taken away that day, so that she could ask for peace. Father threatened that if he refused to do so, he would inform higher authority and would make him responsible for the punishment meted out because of the rebellion. This changed the Captain's mind and he angrily gave up the Indian woman.

Father took her and with great trouble, because of the lack of an interpreter, made her aware of what she should say to her kinsfolk. He gave her things to wear, as best he could by borrowing from the wives of the soldiers a green skirt with a gold band, a petticoat, some white embroidered hose,[15] and a ribboned hat. The Captain, on seeing the eagerness with which Father went about seeking items to clothe that Indian woman, offered an old blouse of his wife and a piece of scarlet cloth; and to dress her even more fittingly Father searched into corners, looking for left-over beads and rosaries and other trinkets that he could find, and the necessary supplies for her journey; finally, he found

15. The Spanish is: "unas blancas labradas."

flint and rock for making fire on the way, and above all, the most important article they gave her was an inlaid cross, which was very beautiful and which she should wear on her neck, with an embossed ribbon which Father took with great faith, since it had served as the ribbon to the key of the depository.[16]

When all necessary things were made ready, Father came and in person invited the Captain to see her safely on her way, because of the danger of being killed by the Indians of these missions, since they always felt their hostility. Concerning all these preparations, there was much chatter and the Captain was the main one. The Indian woman set 20 days to go and visit her tribe and return. God granted that she returned with four of the principal Indians, whom the chief selected. He did not dare to come in person, for he suspected cunning; he gave up the staff and a hide with the insignia of the sun, which the Indians worshipped, as God leads it to be understood.[17] The Indians reached the presidio on October 30; they were going straight to the mission, and were seen accidentally as they passed the presidio. The Captain came out to meet them; when the Indian saw him, he set out toward him on foot and unarmed, and kneeling, extended his hands and offered him the staff and the hide with the insignia of the sun as a sign of peace.

Father was busy at the time and Father Preacher, Ygnacio de Baena and I happened to be present. When Father was informed

---

16. The depository, it seems, was the chest or cabinet in which the sacred vessels and vestments were kept; the Spanish is: "en la llave de el deposito."

17. "As God leads it to be understood"; "it" can refer only to *la insignia* (the insignia or sign) of the sun, as a symbol of peace, as is mentioned farther on. The Spanish is: "y entrego el vaston y una piel con la insignia de el sol a quien adoraban segun se deja entender por Ds. Estos llegaron al Presidio el dia treinta de octubre . . . le entrego el vaston y la piel con la dha insignia de el sol ensenal de paz." The clause "a quien adoraban" is parenthetical.

18. Fr. Ygnacio de Baena (or Ignacio de Bahena) was a visiting missionary from the College of Zacatecas. He died in 1725 at Mission Nuestra Señora del Espíritu Santo while it was still on Garcitas Creek, near Lavaca Bay, a part of Matagorda Bay. Cf. B. Leutenegger and M. A. Habig, *The Zacatecan Missionaries of Texas, 1716-1834* (Austin: Texas State Historical Survey Committee, 1973).

of events, he came quickly, and having arrived in the presence of that Indian woman, he noticed the joy she showed on seeing him. Father asked her if that Indian was the one who had sent her and she answered yes. The joy of the Indian was incredible; he placed his hands on his heart and showed other signs of love. Then we left to give thanks to God, the author of such marvels. We all marched together: we in the midst of the Indians sang the *Te Deum Laudamus.*[19] On arriving at the mission, Fr. Ygnacio de Baena came out with vestments on and with the processional cross. As the bells rang out, we entered the church, singing the psalm *Laudate Dominum omnes gentes,*[20] the oration in thanksgiving, and the Alabado. The Indians were kneeling with hands placed in such a manner that our eyes filled with tears of joy.

When the services were ended, Father brought the Indians to his cell and regaled them in as far as the poverty of religious would allow. They remained there and asked for some articles in the presidio.[21] He placed two of the Indians in the home of one of the soldiers of the mission, and the Indian woman, the wife of the principal Indian, with the ambassadress in the home of another soldier. Two of the main Indians remained with Father in his cell, where they slept alone with Father. In the morning Father knelt down and sang the Alabado. Immediately, the two Indians, one on one side of Father and the other on the other side, knelt also and with hands extended began to sing with Father with great devotion and with great demonstrations of love, as if they wanted to put Father into their hearts, embracing him continually without wanting to let go of his hand.

Many things were proposed to them in favor of peace and of our holy Catholic faith. They agreed to it all with signs of joy and firmness, in such a manner that they seemed to be Indians well instructed. Father treated them again with small gifts he could find, such as a shirt from the infirmary, and underwear of his own. Juan de Castro donated some torn woolen pants and another

---

19. St. Ambrose's hymn, "Holy God, We Praise You."
20. Psalm 116 (117), "Praise the Lord, all you nations" — the shortest of the Psalms.
21. The Spanish is: "pidieron les truxesen los trastes q estaba en el Presidio."

pair of torn cotton pants, and an undervest of green serge; the poor fellow had nothing more to give. Father gave them rosaries for the five Indian captains, two bunches of glass beads, earrings, tobacco, piloncillo,[22] a bag of pinole,[23] and five large knives, the same kind for each captain. With such treats from a poor friar, Father sent them back. On their part the Indians promised for certain that they would return with all their captains unfailingly within twelve days to establish a firm peace.

One regret remains, for those Indians found the captives distributed because of the difficulty of bringing them to the presidio before these Indians came. This serious omission on the part of the Captain came about not because of lack of warning, for Father had urged his plan three or four times. The Captain did not act because it seemed easier to him to return alone than for the Indians to come and ask for peace.

All of this, which has been accomplished and the damages which unfailingly were foreseen by the Indians in their meeting, for the enemy had prepared to come and raze these missions and the presidio, all of this hinged on one thing: would Father become disheartened because of the slim chances he had that the Captain would let him have the Indian woman to carry out his plan.

I was about to forget to tell Your Reverence that when the Indian woman arrived, the Indians already had decided to attack. When she came, their intention was suspended and they entered into a great discussion, which lasted for five days. Finally, the chief, crest-fallen and with bow in hand and absorbed in thought for a good while, suddenly threw the arrow on the ground and with tears in his eyes said: This is good; let us hurry and give the peace.

This is what I have seen and what has happened in my presence. It has given me pleasure to write all these happenings so that Your Reverence may know all that has taken place, and to be a witness as a poor religious. May Christ be with all. Amen.

San Antonio de Valero, November 3, 1723.

---

22. *Piloncillos* were candy bars of brown cane sugar.

23. *Pinole* consisted of ground corn, roasted and sweetened with cane sugar.

Kissing the hand of Your Reverence, your humble subject loves you in the love of Jesus, our Life.

Fray Francisco Hidalgo

(To) Our Rev. Fr. Guardian, Fray Isidro Felis de Espinosa

---

8. Letter of May 29, 1724

In this letter Fr. Hidalgo, missionary in charge of Mission San Antonio de Valero, informs the viceroy that he has appropriately made public a viceregal decree which ordered that no part of the wages allotted to the presidio soldiers by the government be withheld from them. This seems to have been the last letter sent by Fr. Hidalgo from Mission San Antonio; and it indicates that he was still there at the end of May, 1724. Not long afterwards he retired to Mission San Juan Bautista on the Mexican side of the Rio Grande; and there he died on November 6, 1726. The original Spanish letter is in the Biblioteca Nacional, Mexico City; a microfilm copy is at the Academy of American Franciscan History, Washington, D. C., and a transcript from the latter is in RLSJ.

Fr. Francisco Hidalgo, apostolic preacher, ex-Guardian of Santa Cruz, notary of the Holy Office, founder of the three apostolic Colleges of this New Spain of the regular Observance of our Father St. Francis and of ten missions for the pagans, I certify in the manner in which it should be by right and as of this date of May 28, 1724, in this Presidio of San Antonio de Valero, which with the knowledge of His Majesty is located in this place where a testimony was made public of a letter written by the Most Excellent Lord Viceroy, the Governor and Captain General of this new Spain, dated in the city of Mexico on February 27 of said year, when the soldiers and their Captain were together in that presidio. The contents of that letter tells of past practices (as it is said), when in some of the presidios of this land the salary of the soldiers was reduced by taking a portion which His Majesty had determined should be paid to them.

We advise you, Most Excellent Lord Viceroy, that as of October 1, 1722, this abuse was to stop; this testimony I certify in agreement with that original letter for having it made up and published and placed in custody on a tablet about 1½ vara from the floor so that this testimony be preserved and at all times be kept from destruction. All this is certified for the Most Excellent Lord Viceroy of this new Spain. That this be evident, I present this in this Mission of San Antonio de Valero on May 29, 1724.

Fr. Francisco Hidalgo